Marketing and PR on a Shoestring

D0084257

Marketing and PR ... on a Shoestring

Getting customers and keeping them ... without breaking the bank

Philip R. Holden and Nick Wilde

BLOOMSBURY

First published in Great Britain 2007 by A & C Black Publishers Ltd

This edition published by

Bloomsbury Publishing Plc
50 Bedford Square, London WC1B 3PD

British Library Cataloguing in Publication Data

A CIP record for this book is available from the British Library.

ISBN: 978-1-4081-3988-2

This book is produced using paper that is made from wood grown in managed, sustainable forests. It is natural, renewable and recyclable. The logging and manufacturing processes conform to the environmental regulations of the country of origin.

Design by Fiona Pike, Pike Design, Winchester
Typeset by RefineCatch Ltd, Bungay, Suffolk
Printed and bound by CPI Group (UK) Ltd, Croydon, CR0 4YY

CONTENTS

PREFACE

There is always a chance that you are the kind of reader who starts at the beginning and works your way through a book. If not, then you probably aren't reading this.

If you are, then we'd like to make a couple of observations.

The first is that this is a book about marketing. So, if you picked it up thinking it was going to give you 100 ways to 'close that sale', think again. Marketing doesn't work like that.

The second is to say that the first line of the preceding paragraph wasn't quite right. This is a book about *doing* marketing. We therefore respectfully suggest that you read this book with pen and paper in hand and your PC turned on, since you should be *doing* as much as you are *reading about* marketing.

Actually, there is a third point to make.

While we have written this to teach people how to market their business 'on a shoestring', no-one ever got richer just by reading. Once you start *doing* what we suggest, you'll effectively teach yourself. If you do, this book will have worked.

Wisdom is knowing what to do next.

Skill is knowing how to do it.

Virtue is doing it.

– Phil Holden & Nick Wilde

A NOTE ABOUT THIS EDITION

Not much has changed since 2007. Has it?

Well, governments around the world come and go (some willingly). Facebook grows to half a billion users. The recession trundles on. TV becomes 3DTV. Maybe some things have changed.

But, we believe, on balance what follows is as good a guide to small business marketing as you'll get.

For example, we've never claimed that there is a simple solution to all business woes or that you can somehow surf the wave of the latest boom (or bust). What we do claim instead is that you can build *your own* marketing plan that can succeed whatever the economic or business climate.

To be honest though, we have said very little here about online marketing. One of the reasons for this is that for small businesses (on a shoestring) the Web often promises far more than it can deliver. And it often creates as many challenges as it does solutions.

The other reason is that online marketing is dealt with in another book we're rather keen on. *Virtually Free Marketing* (by Philip Holden) was published in 2009 and by the time you read this a new, improved version will be imminent or in the bookshops.

It's likely that the next edition of *this* book will be very different. But then again, we bet that the principles in the next couple of chapters will last a good few years. So we invite your responses and ideas through our website *www.pleasewalkonthegrass.com*, via Twitter (@pwotg) and if you can find us individually on Facebook and LinkedIn.

Small business owners who take on the challenges of this book will still find the future changing. But they will be the ones changing it for their own customers and so they will be relatively unconcerned by the 'next big thing'. With a little luck – the next big thing could be their business.

Philip Holden
July 2011

ACKNOWLEDGEMENTS

Dedicated to my Dad and all he's taught me. And to my ever supportive wife and children – all wise beyond their years.
– Phil

To the memory of Stuart Wilde, who inspired me in so many ways, and to my Dad for introducing me to business.
– Nick

Philip R. Holden

Phil is an experienced marketer, having worked in marketing since leaving University College London with a degree in Anthropology. He is also an experienced teacher, trainer and consultant, having run his own marketing communications business before joining Charities Aid Foundation where he helped launch the CharityCard. He is the programme director for the MA in Marketing Communications and devised the marketing component of the MBA in SME Management at the University of Greenwich. He is a researcher with a PhD that is seemingly taking forever and he is a founder of *www.pleasewalkonthegrass.com*, the creative challenge consultancy. He lives in Kent with his wife and children.

Nick Wilde

Nick's career started with a degree in International Marketing and he has worked in the holiday industry, market research, the food import industry and, most recently, in education. As a fluent Spanish speaker, he is an experienced consultant and educator internationally, having worked in the US, Mexico, Argentina and

ACKNOWLEDGEMENTS

Spain as well as developing links in other European countries, including Scandinavia. He is an expert in sports marketing, advising on branding, merchandise and development programmes in the UK and abroad. He acted as marketing consultant to the Charlton Athletic United States Soccer Academy (CAUSSA). He is visiting lecturer in Sports Marketing both on the highly acclaimed MBA Football Industries Management at University of Liverpool (where he will shortly complete his PhD) and at Gdansk University of Technology. He is a founder of *www.pleasewalkonthegrass.com*, the creative challenge consultancy, and lives in London.

1 WHAT'S SO DIFFERENT ABOUT SMALL BUSINESS?

If you've ever picked up a book about marketing or business before, you're probably familiar with the kind of text book that starts with definitions. Maybe it then goes on to tell you some of the history of marketing. Next, it will go on to regale you with tales of the marketing success that big, often global, companies have enjoyed. Some of the more entertaining books also tell you about some of the *failures* of large companies, which allow us a certain frisson of pleasure because we're sure we wouldn't make those kinds of mistakes.

This isn't that kind of book.

You can be small *and* successful

If you are starting or running a small business it's certain that you have in mind one of the following objectives:

1. to survive
2. to stabilise
3. to grow

And, although these might also apply to larger companies, the effects of success and failure are far more keenly felt by you and people like you and in your position.

So, we wanted to start off by explaining why it's misleading to think of marketing, and indeed business, in terms of big companies – as most business books tend to.

The fact is that you will never have the resources to compete directly with the biggest brands in the world. But our point is that you shouldn't do that anyway. It's not that they are successful and you're not; they're just different. Why should this matter? Well, first of all it shows the small business owner that there is a big ocean out there and although there may be whales (and very big sharks), there are also minnows (do they live in the sea?). And, importantly, many of the minnows are doing very well, thank you very much.

Whatever industry you think you are in, there will always be competitors that are bigger than you and many that are the same size or smaller. So how do *they* survive in the same water as the giants? They are not as famous, they don't make as much noise, or as much profit. They clearly don't have the same budget for marketing and PR. The answer (to continue the fishy analogy) is that they occupy different ecosystems. The minnows don't fight the shark for its food ... sometimes they *are* its food ... but they don't go head-to-head over the local scuba divers.

Actually, there are quite a number of industries in which the small fry out-number the big fish – and where their total customer base is larger. These are often trades, like plumbing or printing, or professions, like solicitors and doctors, but also restaurants. They're typically industries where it is usual to be a sole trader (no pun intended) or a very small business, and frequently they provide a service to a very local or specialised group of customers. Therefore, the small owner-managed store is actually offering a different product and service to the big name stores. They are different propositions and their marketing should, therefore, be different too. Of course, in one sense they are competing, but the smaller company should have a clear idea of what it's best at. Only then can it begin to find (and keep) the customers that rightly belong to it.

Small and medium-sized enterprises (SMEs) exist in a different dimension of time and space. They have a different relationship with the world, which is both a difficulty and an opportunity. It's a difficulty because most of what we understand about business (including what we learn from most business books and business schools) is based on big businesses, which operate in *their* own time and space. It's an opportunity, however, because by understanding their true place, small businesses can move quickly and effectively into a new space in the market and succeed – often before anyone knows that this 'market space' exists.

DIY marketing?

Let's look at the UK DIY market and the big players in it. B&Q's retail profit, which in 2011 was roughly £83 million, is generated by around 300 stores (as well as online selling and some other sources which we'll ignore), which means they're making roughly £276,000 profit per store. We also know that they have roughly 2.5 million square metres of retail space.[1] So, their profit works out as £33.20 per square metre . . . per year. Put like that, it's not so impressive is it? Of course their turnover is much greater than their profit – they have to pay for the stores, personnel and product amongst other things.

So, you want to work out your 'merchandising intensity'?

For an interesting comparison, if you're in retailing, work out how effective your store is. To do this, add up your turnover and make a note of your net profit.

Next, work out the area of your store that is used for selling, remembering to include counters, display areas, changing rooms — in fact anywhere the customers can see or go. (In most shops, it's pretty simple: multiply width by depth. You can use square metres or feet, but stick to one type of measurement.)

Finally, divide each of the financial numbers in turn by the area. Are you more or less efficient than B&Q?

(Hint: you can also use this technique to see if you are using office space effectively and whether a move to bigger or better offices can be justified.)

Now there are two kinds of small, local hardware and DIY store. There are the stores run by people who think maybe they should find out about this marketing lark and perhaps go out and buy a book or take a course or just observe the big competitors like B&Q so that they can find out what they are doing and try and copy them ... and there are the rest; the ones like you (having read the first few pages of this book).

The second kind of store owner should now at least have an inkling that they can claim a unique position in the marketplace, that they offer a service no-one else can. These are the people who understand that they already have customers and that (this is the big one) **those customers define their marketplace**. It will come as no surprise to you to know that it is the latter kind of store owner that we believe will succeed.

Of course, there are exceptions; if you have a rapidly growing business with more customers knocking on your door than you can cope with — and into which someone is prepared to pour millions of pounds worth of investment — this book may not quite meet your needs. However, if you want to get into that position in the first place . . .

What kind of reader are you?

It's a pretty safe bet that if you picked up this book, it was as much the 'Shoestring' bit that attracted you as the 'Marketing and PR'. So you've already accepted that you don't have much of a budget.

One of the principles of this book is that you can't shout louder than everyone, but you can whisper in the right ear. Knowledge really is power. What that actually means is that it's useless complaining that you have a limited budget. Pretty much everyone in business has to face this fact. You may feel you have no budget at all, but you still have resources and you have to establish priorities for using them. You'll never have enough money to do *everything* all of the time: let's face it, if you had several million in your pocket what would you do? (Moving to the Caribbean and living off the interest springs to mind.)

You may also feel that you have no time to devote to devising a marketing plan, let alone rethinking your 'business philosophy'. It's a cry we've heard from many a small business manager. But the fact is that you're in business and you have to earn money week in, week out. As a result, you need to get customers (*to survive*) and, we suggest, you have to keep them too. Or perhaps you're thinking about starting in business and you want to know how you're going to attract enough business to make the kind of profit you feel you need (*to stabilise*)? Of course, you may also want to do great things, build the company, sell it and make your way to the Caribbean (*to grow*, of course!).

We can only suggest what we feel is the right way of achieving this. And rather than giving you a long list of 'golden rules' to follow, we would rather you understood why our ideas might work.

Important numbers . . .

So what should *you* monitor? Actually, there is a lot of academic work done on retailing[2] (as an example of just one industry your company might be in) that shows how you can measure the performance of the products you stock, stores (in terms of area) and employees and come up with a few very important 'metrics' – key figures that tell you how you are doing. You could also look at one of the companion books in this series – *Boosting Sales* by Bob Gorton – for a detailed guide to the numbers that you need to keep watching and which could form part of your business and marketing objectives.

But customers and customers alone are the source of your income (and therefore of your profit). Almost everything else in the business (the production of widgets, employment of people to make widgets and, of course, the promotion of the widgets and door-to-door delivery of the widgets) has a cost and so can impact on your profitability. That much is obvious.

So, anything designed to increase income has to be related to customers in three simple ways:

1. **getting more customers to buy from you,** *or*
2. **getting them to buy more from you,** *or*
3. **getting them to pay more for what they buy**

We'll discuss pricing in a later chapter, but for the moment the point is clear. There may be much about your business you cannot change, but what you can and should look at changing is your interaction with customers so that in some way you're able to achieve one of these three simple objectives. And, bearing in mind that everything you do has a cost, the effect of one of the above three aims has to be greater than the costs of achieving it. So we should add a fourth point to the above . . .

4. **. . . profitably!**
And that, as they say, is marketing.

It's all about doing something to (with, for?) customers that will get more of them to buy more, more frequently and all at a profit. And you won't know if you can do that unless you have a pretty good idea of what customers are like, what they want, how much they'll pay and so on. More things to monitor and record.

So far we've managed to avoid the question that all marketing books start with:

What is marketing?

Actually, we're quite proud of this since it marks out this book as different (which you'll discover later is an important principle in marketing) and also because most definitions are pretty useless. The problem is that once you have a definition, you either think you understand marketing or, just as likely, you start finding exceptions to the rule and lose faith in marketing itself. We won't waste words, then, on a history of marketing or an exegesis of some learned institute's definition. If you want that, the first chapter of many text books will oblige.

However, if you need a definition to keep referring back to, here's one of the best:

> *'Marketing is the whole company seen from the point of view of the customer.'*[3]

It can't really be put any more clearly. Marketing is simply about putting customers at the centre of everything you do.

As we shall see later in the book, that doesn't mean you give all customers everything they want. That would be suicidal for your company. But marketing is a way of thinking about your business that makes you consider what customers will buy from you *before* you decide what to provide them with. Any other definition is simply an unnecessary elaboration.

Keep in mind, then, that when we discuss marketing in this book, we're not talking about selling or advertising; we're talking about your whole company or organisation looked at with the customer in mind.

Growing overheads instead of the business

Starting off in business, a close friend was working from the converted basement of his house.

Of course it wasn't ideal and he quickly took on a brand new unit in a business park with some ten times the space he'd been used to. A very prestigious address and a comfortable place to welcome the big, well-off clients that would come as the business expanded.

As it happened, in the five years the company operated there, it did expand a little but only about five clients ever visited. Clients paying considerable amounts of money for your services expect *you* to visit *them*.

Unfortunately, the new offices proved to be a financial millstone and when the business stopped expanding (and in fact had to shrink), the high rent contributed to the need to downsize even more rapidly and, eventually, wind the company up.

The story tells us three things.

1. That the trappings of success need to be earned by a business. You have to be supremely confident, and maybe lucky, to take on new premises in the hope that it will result in new customers – and such expansion isn't necessarily a good thing. Any investment needs to be justified in terms of its effect on the business.

2. That even investments which appear to impact on customers in a positive way may not, and need to be tested.

3. And that, sadly, even if you think you understand marketing, there's no guarantee of success. The company belonged to one of the authors of this book.

Investing in your customers

Marketing for small businesses is about investing in customers, and like every investment it should generate more than it costs. We should also add that, once you look upon marketing as an investment, you can compare its performance with other possible investments such as the suggestion you move to larger premises, or acquiring new machinery, shop-fittings, staff, telephones or any of the hundreds of other things that compete for your resources and that, sometimes, are bought purely for vanity's sake.

We're not pleading a special case for marketing so, in the later chapters, you won't find us recommending that you spend your advertising budget on 'raising awareness' or 'building your profile'. Even though these are (quite legitimate) long term aims that large companies can afford to pursue, they're not appropriate for a small business operating on a shoestring.

> You want to survive, stabilise or grow and you can do this by achieving marketing objectives 1 or 2 or 3 (*and* 4) above. That's all.

But I want to be famous . . .

There is, of course, the problem of vanity, as mentioned above. It goes without saying that you want your company to be a success, but don't let this get in the way of making sound business decisions. Your objectives should still be to survive, stabilise and grow.

But what if I don't have any customers?

If you don't have customers, you'll need to find some. Quickly. Without customers, there is no business. If you're in this position and you are relying on the business to pay next month's mortgage, we have some very good advice for you. Get a job.

There is, simply, no way to get a new and sustainable business off the ground in a few weeks. Every successful entrepreneur we've ever met or read about set up his or her business over months, sometimes years, very often as they were holding down another job. Even so, a true 'marketing' company (that focuses on customers first and always) demands a lot of time and effort to establish. If you now have to delay the launch of your new venture, look upon it as valuable thinking and planning time. A good marketing plan (that is, one that works for the company, rather than just *sounds* convincing) demands time.

Although we've said that marketing focuses on customers, your plan to increase the number flocking to your door can't focus on them to the exclusion of all else. Your plan needs to also look at the company and everything that it does that may influence the customer – what's known as the 'value chain', which we look at in more detail later on – not the least of which is the product or service you hope to sell. If this isn't right, even if you entice customers to try you (you can, after all, promise them the earth), they may not return. So we ask you to start from the position that you want to attract customers *and* keep them. We'll look at this in even more detail in Chapters 5 and 6.

If, however, you want to start off in business (or you want to rescue a business that already exists) and you'd like to enjoy the journey, read on. As many as one in four of us are likely to be thinking of starting a business and, perhaps just as crucially, new companies that go bust are more likely to do so in the first two years of trading[4]. Even in comparatively benign trading conditions, 1% of *all* businesses will go broke in the next two years.

It's unlikely you'll have money to splash around. Even if you did, you'd still need to spend it effectively. Your business will start off doing most things on a shoestring but, as it grows, the principles of marketing based on a thorough understanding of your customers and what they need – the principles of this book – will be the same, no matter how much money you spend.

Let's get three things straight

In this chapter, we want to introduce you to some of the key principles of this book. They are that:

1. **small companies are different from big companies**
2. **all products have a service element to them (and if they don't, they should)**
3. **the marketing strategies that small companies should use vary according to customers and markets, not products or industry sector**

Let's explain here . . .

> **Principle 1.** Small companies are different. Many business writers regard them in the same way that the comedian Graham Norton regards children in his famous quip: 'they're like real people ... only smaller'. But we believe that small businesses are *not* miniature big businesses.

A problem for most small businesses is that the so-called 'key implementers' (the people who have to make the strategy work) cannot divide themselves into CEO, director of Human Resources, Finance Director and so on. When you're writing a marketing plan, it's very handy to be able to ignore issues of finance and employing people but, in our experience, it feels wrong. If you need six new salespeople to make your plan work, then you must consider how to employ them and how to pay them.

In most companies (and we mean most companies), all these management functions co-exist in one or two people. Day-to-day decisions overlap all functional areas of the business and it's not simply that it's difficult to distinguish between them; in truth, there *is no distinction*. Big business administration depends on the cost benefits of specialisation; small businesses usually can't. The lesson of this is that if you make a decision about anything, it should be in the best interests of the company as a whole. And usually that means looking after the interests of the customers (remember – the only source of income).

Any business that relies on customers (so, all of them!) should consider some of the other factors which will impact on those customers. Anything in your business (and in others) which helps to deliver value to your customers is therefore worthy of attention. This is the 'value chain' we mentioned above.

To take the most straightforward example of the value chain, you can't allow your hard work in building and selling your products or services to be let down by a late delivery or even a non-delivery. Can you really not be more precise than giving your customers a three-hour slot for delivery? The delivery of your product at a time that suits your customer is a source of value to them. Looking up and down the value chain, you'll see many factors that impact on your customers' ability to enjoy your product. If you start to try and manage these, then you change your company's orientation still more. From making sofas or photocopiers, you might find that you start having to learn how to sell loans and maintenance – or why not interior design and office planning?

As the owner of a 'marketing' company, in our sense, you should frequently be asking yourself the question 'what business am I in?'

How about...?

...taking some time now to think about the 'strategic' plans you have developed for your business, either recently or in the past. Were they simply copies of other people's? Were they no more than ideas for promoting your company?

If you're in the midst of running a company, taking time to think is NOT a luxury. You have our permission to book yourself time out of the factory – we recommend at least half a day a month – to go where you can't be disturbed. Switch the phones off and make notes, start doodling or recording your thoughts and just think.

Our starter question is 'Where is the business going in the next 12 months?'. 'How do you know?'

Strategies for success

When you start to ask very searching questions of your business and its direction, you're dealing with strategy. Strategy is one of the most over-used words in business. For our purposes, we'll use the definition of strategy that a very knowledgeable colleague once gave us: 'It's anything that is long term and important'. It doesn't need to be any more complicated than that.

This leads us on to . . .

> **Principle 2.** All products have a service element and if they don't, they should. In other words, a physical product is *never* enough to get and keep customers.

This second principle may seem a little obscure at this point. Bear with us again.

Marketing people frequently talk about 'products'. And that is fine as long as we understand that they don't mean products in the everyday sense. For a marketer, a product is *anything* that can be offered to customers for their consideration. So products are not only physical goods but they are also *everything else* that customers buy along the way.

It's worth thinking about this for a moment. If someone is in the business of selling windows, then the fact that his company is ISO9000 approved might be very important. He may be convinced that the windows meet all the manufacturing criteria he can think of; they are well made and they perform excellently. Now, if only he could get the fitters to do *their* job!

Thinking more broadly about product leads us to understand that the window fitters who don't wipe their feet or fail to clean up after themselves are a significant part of the product. It simply doesn't work to say to an irate customer, 'Ah, but the fitters are freelance, you pay them separately.' The business owner made the sale, he has to deliver satisfaction or . . . or well, dissatisfaction?

Strategy for the second generation

Taking over a family business is never easy.

The Watergate Bay Hotel on Cornwall's North Coast is a landmark on the road out of Newquay, one of the region's liveliest holiday resorts. To see the hotel's greatest asset, you only have to gaze from the terrace of its newly refurbished bar – two miles of sand busy with holiday makers and beautiful breaking surf.

The hotel had been in the Ashworth family for thirty years, but the holiday business had changed a great deal during that time. Fortunately, Will, the youngest son, took on the challenge, following the example of his brother, Henry, who had bought the beach ice-cream hut and shop and was busy turning them into a centre for surfing and the other 'extreme' sports that had become so popular in the last few years.

For a while, Will, like many second-generation entrepreneurs, felt lost in someone else's business. Then came the realisation that to make the hotel work and to begin to enjoy what he did, he would have to make it his own. Henry's 'Extreme Academy' provided the inspiration.

Why couldn't he establish a resort that gave people everything they needed to enjoy the beach lifestyle? The vision was a 'ski resort on a beach'.

Finding your own way

We're conscious that we've asked you lots of questions and you came to this book looking for answers. Don't worry, they're coming!

The problem, as we have said, is that there isn't just *one* answer. While the principles of business can be codified and written down, each successful small business is slightly different.

This brings us to our third principle.

> **Principle 3.** The 'one strategy fits all' approach doesn't help. Most business books either offer one or two examples of small business practice without analysis or, if they deal with them at all, add a small business chapter as an afterthought.
>
> People go into business for different reasons and expect different rewards. Likewise, different kinds of business have different opportunities and constraints. Strategies therefore must be different.

The typical small business (particularly when it starts up) exists in a space where it's difficult to see how many customers there are, how much they'll spend or what the competition is like. We hope that, as you read this book, you'll begin to get a better sense of your own position.

In the meantime, following our third principle, we want to give you some idea of a 'route map' for your strategy. For many businesses, the starting position is the recognition of an opportunity or the desire to do something with the entrepreneur's perceived abilities (see below).

In this situation there is very little hard evidence but a lot of 'gut feelings', some of which can be very useful. Some of these feelings

First thoughts on starting a business

are about the external environment and some are about the 'internal' competencies of the business founders. You might well have an instinct for a successful business, and the following chapters will enable you to investigate the market and decide exactly what you are going to do about it. It might also make you realise that, in fact, your idea needs some more thought and you'd better revise your plans before it's too late.

Some research[5] published a few years ago summarised the six factors that motivated business start ups. The key points, as you'd expect, were that all entrepreneurs wanted their business to succeed and give them a return on their investment. What was interesting, though, was that the desire to create something of their own and to have a measure of autonomy were just as important.

The same research identified the main factors that restrained business start-ups. These were dominated by a lack of skills, including management and finance as well as marketing.

Happiness is a hairy potato

When we run courses for small business managers, we use an exercise that forces them to think about what their own personal aims or values are before going on to think about their company's aims.

In an exercise of free thinking, we invite managers of SMEs to forget their business problems and consider instead what makes them happy — or rather what things in their life would contribute to their happiness in the long term. The results end up looking like excessively hairy potatoes, sometimes multi-coloured, but they give us all pause for thought.

In the diagram overleaf you can see how one manager approached the task.

While almost everyone wrote down things relating to their work, they were also encouraged to include family, friends, their health, hobbies and aspirations. For most people, this led to a reappraisal of their priorities and an understanding of the close link between their work and other things that they valued. Money, although it was mentioned, was only one part of a complex mix of motivations. For the majority, money was a means to an end.

A sense of purpose

Whatever else you need in your business, you must have a sense of the reason why the business exists at all. You need to spend time understanding the key principles of running a small business which, while they constrain your opportunities, can also renew and rejuvenate your approach, if they are properly understood.

Remember that your values and objectives are the vital 'key implementers' of your business's strategy. If you have partners, so are theirs. However, this is not an instruction to go and implement every clichéd marketing initiative you've ever studied or heard about; nor is it a quick fix that involves splashing a few adverts

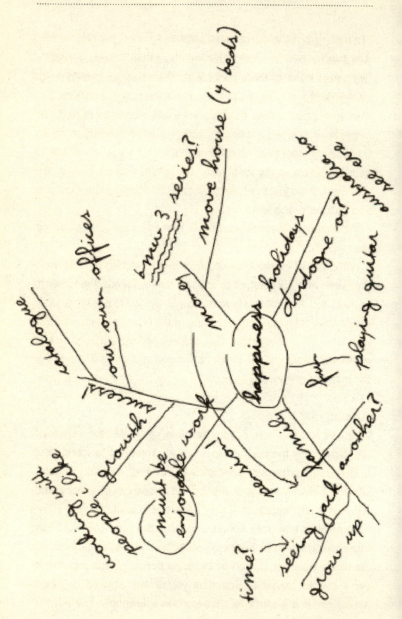

around. The approach we are urging is based on re-visualising the place your small business occupies in the world and inventing your own unique strategy to make your position profitable and sustainable.

Thinking laterally

Will Ashworth's vision for the Watergate Bay Hotel was simple – more than just a bed and food whilst on holiday, the hotel *was* the holiday – but the consequences of seeing it through rather than just paying lip service were immense.

Will realised that he would have to invest in the buildings, facilities and service to create a real destination. Over five years, more than £3 million was invested in building a new wing of four-star sea-view bedrooms and upgrading the reception area, restaurant and public areas.

Although Will admits that money is more of a motivation for him than for some family members, it was not the only concern. Profit was simply necessary to pay for the changes to the business.

When asked about the 'purpose' of the Watergate Bay Hotel, Will answers that it is complex. 'It is not only about making the most of this business – making it the very best it can be; there are a host of other values that are important to the customers we aim to attract,' he says.

The resort is working to develop sustainable holiday homes by sourcing produce from small local and organic producers and to reduce its energy consumption. Sustainability is a key factor and Will is looking into a biomass generator that could supply 80% of its heating.

The aim is also to maximise the positive effect it has on the local economy. Only a few years ago the hotel closed completely for six weeks every winter. Now it is open all year and provides full-time employment for 80 local people.

Take action now

Throughout this book, we want to you *do* rather than simply read. So, pen in hand, try the following:

1. Write down, in one concise sentence, what business you're in.
2. Now try that again, this time making sure that you describe your business from your customers' point of view.
3. Next, sketch out the 'value chain'. Include all the things outside your control that the customer has to go through to enjoy your product or service.
4. Make a note of your objectives. Do you want to survive, stabilise or grow?

5. Try the 'hairy potato' exercise and work out what you want out of your business. (If you have business partners, ask them to do the same.)
6. Now go back and rethink the answers to questions 1 to 4. These may have to change to meet the aims and objectives of you (and your co-owners).

Opening soon! The Bland Sandwich Shop

If you put up this notice, you're going to turn your customers away. The truth is we could take you to many shops that *should* have this sign up! Let's face it, many of those that make the sandwiches on the premises have mountains of 'catering-pack' ham, cheddar cheese and tuna mayonnaise. Hardly any of them are ever going to win prizes. Is this really what people want from a sandwich?

To refresh your understanding of customers, it is useful to consider that frequent sandwich buyers don't buy the same thing every day: they want a bit of variety. It isn't just about price or a straightforward value calculation (i.e. bigger = better). So why aren't there more exciting choices? Why not make buying a sandwich more of an event?

Try some new recipes and let your customers sample them. Make sure that even the cheese in your cheese

and pickle sandwich is one of the best that you can find
... then ring the changes, still using top-quality
ingredients, every week.

Notes / References

1. You can find most of these figures at the website for B&Q's parent company, *www.kingfisher.co.uk*.

2. Ring, L.J. et al. (2002). 'The Strategic Resource Management (SRM) model revisited', *International Journal of Retail and Distribution Management*. Volume 30, Number 11, pages 544–561.

3. Attributed to Peter Drucker back in the 1960s.

4. Cressy, R. (2006) 'Why Do Most Firms Die Young?', *Small Business Economics*, Volume 26, 103–116.

5. Mazzarol, T. et al. (1998). *Creativity drives the dream: an empirical analysis of the factors motivating business start-ups*, ICSB World Conference, Singapore.

2 FIRST STEPS IN THE PLANNING PROCESS

Having considered why you are in business, and indeed what kind of business you *want* to be in, in this chapter we'll look at how you can start developing an outline of a distinctive plan for your business. Starting with your broader 'corporate' objectives you'll then consider the best ways of achieving them. We'll also look at how you can choose a realistic strategic direction based on the basic alternatives we propose and by setting your business within a model devised especially for small businesses. Focusing on your marketplace by visualising the marketplace in terms of customer numbers and their buying patterns, will mean that you'll be able to consider more innovative strategic options. Finally, we'll also look a how to start writing a marketing plan.

Can you explain what the opportunities are for your business?

Most successful business ventures are a result of entrepreneurs spotting an opportunity in a marketplace they know well. You need, therefore, to be able to show what these opportunities are and to try and put figures to them. If, for example, you have designed a new recycling bin which can be sold to local authorities and private individuals, get some feedback about the *need* for your new product. You could ask householders about their current recycling habits and their views on what would encourage them to recycle more. The fact that 40% of all households are 'interested in composting' is a start; ballpark figures are okay at this stage. Not having any figures at all is very worrying.

What is the trading environment?

Part of the marketing planning process is to understand how your business is affected by the current trends in the market and where your competitors are. Markets can really only do the following:

1. **fall**
2. **stagnate**
3. **rise**

For each of these, there are two further measures to consider:

1. **value (the amount of money the goods are sold for)**
2. **volume (the total number of units sold)**

These are simply measures that indicate the current business climate. If the number of suppliers remains the same, a falling market will become more competitive. If there are also new entrants to that market, competition will ratchet up even further. Prices will probably be falling too.

Business objectives

It's now time to start writing out some objectives for your business. You already have a feel for what is acceptable to you – what kind of business you want and where you would like it to go. Add to this some basic information about the economy and the market, and you can estimate some figures.

> I'd like to grow this company's turnover from £60,000 to £100,000, but I know the market for building and home improvements is only growing at 2% per annum.

What then will be the key business objectives for your organisation, based on an assessment of the market, which is either stagnant, rising or falling? Also, does this business objective meet your personal objectives? What effect does it have on the amount you need (want?) to pay yourself, for example?

Chapter 3 will offer more guidance on these points, but there's also a lot of free information that you can tap in to. For example the accounting firm Grant Thornton (www.grant-thornton.co.uk) produces regular reports on various business sectors. Its January 2006 summary of the retail trade over the previous Christmas[1] showed that average results were up 1.1% on the same period a year before. However, while some sub-sectors had enjoyed greater growth ('electricals', for instance, were up over 3%), others had declined. 'Household and homeware' sales had declined by over 7%.

Simple, accessible summaries like this give you real food for thought. Can you achieve the average result (and, in effect, stay still), or can you beat it? If your sector is declining by 7%, should you really budget on the basis of even modest growth?

It would be nigh-on impossible for your figures to be completely exact, no matter how big your company, and even if you have very good historical data from which to forecast. But at this stage *any* figures help reduce uncertainty and will enable you to monitor your progress.

A model for *your* business

Once you have an idea of the trading environment, you need to get a feel for how you can develop a marketing plan tailored to your business, based on customers and their needs.

In our experience, the difficulties small businesses have in discovering customers' needs and organising the business around them are heavily influenced by the sheer number of customers (and potential customers) that have to be dealt with and the value of transactions involved. Broadly speaking, we can map businesses on the two axes shown below (which we're proud to unveil as the Holden-Wilde (HW) matrix).

The idea is simply to start thinking about where your customers are, how many there are and whether each transaction they undertake with you is of a high or low value to them. As a start-up business, how many customers do you think are out there? How much do they spend?

	Number of customers	
	Few customers	**Many customers**
High value	**A** Not many customers but spend a lot	**B** Many customers who buy high value goods or who spend a lot on their transactions
Low value	**C** There are few customers who also spend very little	**D** There are lots of customers but who spend very little but frequently.

Value of transactions

Most businesses think that they are at position D, where there are plenty of customers, but they just don't seem to buy often. Sometimes businesses think of themselves at A, but underestimate their competition. However, you could well be in position B or C but you are 'sharing' the customers with many businesses similar to your own. This does not represent an opportunity. From position C do you then move across the grid and attempt to get more customers or move up the grid and find more valuable customers? That's a strategic decision.

Now before you all start composing e-mails of complaint that this is wholly unrealistic for all kinds of reasons, we *know* this model is very subjective. You have to use your judgement to gauge where you are and what your customers' perceptions are. We know — honestly. But we think it's worth persevering to make you investigate the *reality* of your market rather than rely on sweeping, and largely unfounded, marketing folklore.

We've come across numerous business people who sincerely believe they offer 'the best' product. It's actually quite endearing and you might expect that every entrepreneur believes in his or her own product. However, an attempt to take a more analytical, objective view of your business usually pays dividends.

While we are aware of the danger of making sweeping generalisations about business, here are some examples of the kinds of businesses/products/markets that might fall into one of the quadrants of the Holden-Wilde matrix.

But bear in mind that all of this is relative: a frequent purchaser of luxury cars may view the purchase of a small 'run-about' for the nanny as a minor and infrequent purchase unworthy of much decision time! Let's just say that it is precisely in these kinds of 'exceptions' that small businesses discover so-called 'niche' opportunities. To continue this example, a company selling

RELATIVELY	Few customers Infrequent purchase	Many customers More frequent purchase
Large transactions (from the point of view of the customer)	Large plant and machinery Custom built kitchens Very 'high-end' luxury cars	Standardised equipment Kitchen appliances 'Mass market' cars
Small transactions (from the point of view of the customer)	Emergency products & services Small, specialist components and services Information and 'know-how'	Everyday office consumables Groceries, corner shop Impulse purchases

expensive cars to the very wealthy could make considerable profit sourcing other less expensive cars (perhaps with a partner company) to meet such needs. The likelihood is that the purchaser of these smaller cars would be less sensitive to the price than those for whom it represents a 'big deal'. This is an example of 'share of pocket' (or wallet) rather than 'share of market', since by conventional analysis the company has moved into a different market sector.

This is a useful measure to bear in mind and it may form part of your marketing objectives. As a very small company you won't be aiming for a significant percentage share of a market, but you can get near to a 100% share of certain customers — and that's enough to make a very comfortable living. Think about how you could position your business in the grid to reach those people.

But what does it all mean?

The HW matrix is based partly on the kinds of purchase decisions customers are making. As a result, it leads directly to a consideration of the ways in which you can support that decision making and the opportunities you have to do so – in other words, your marketing strategy. Furthermore, because we are also considering the value of the transaction, there is also a suggestion of the kind of marketing investment needed for different customers. To illustrate this, we've taken just one business area and positioned four different businesses (A, B, C and D) in the grid.

As you can see, the categories don't quite fit perfectly. For example, you could argue that firm B should appear further to the left since people don't buy burglar alarms very frequently. However it's undoubtedly a mass market with DIY alternatives available at very low cost so there are, potentially, many customers out there.

RELATIVELY	Few customers Infrequent purchase	Many customers More frequent purchase	Marketing approach
Large transactions	A: Specialises in very high security for businesses	B: Offers alarm systems and monitoring, both commercial and domestic	Long-term relationship approach Service excellence positioning
Small transactions	C: Emergency locksmith	D: Key cutting, retailer of locks, chains, hardware	Emphasise convenience No-nonsense positioning

Marketing approach

Positioned as specialist Need to be 'on the short-list' Easy to find when a decision is to be made

Positioned as offering good value Visibility, easy to find

Holden-Wilde matrix applied to the security industry

The point is that, in order to make a decision about where you are on the grid, you need some information and that information is *relative* to other companies, or other groups of customers or your customers' other needs or purchases.

If you were in the security market, you'd have to make decisions about which direction you intended to go in. Are you getting the basics right? Do you chase more customers making more frequent purchases, or do you try and move 'up market' and go for higher value, possibly less frequent purchases?

If you wanted to think creatively about your industry and what you could do that was different from the competition, you need only play around with your position on the grid. For example, what could you do as an emergency locksmith that dealt only with the highest value customers? Is there perhaps an opportunity for a highly tailored security service available 'over the counter', say through a large retailer?

On the next page is a blank matrix for you to copy and fill in.

Bear in mind as you try to fill out the HM matrix that there is *no* one right way to do it. All businesses are different and the purpose of the matrix is to help you realise and emphasise those differences.

Some versions of your matrix will seem very narrowly focused (on your customers, say), while others will seem to identify many competitors. Don't worry: you are developing your insight into your business and your customers and identifying a 'market space' you can exploit.

The marketing plan

Now we're nearing the moment. Yes, it's that time when we are going to ask you to write a marketing plan.

Start your plan with a statement about your business; a combination of your beliefs and values (along with those of fellow

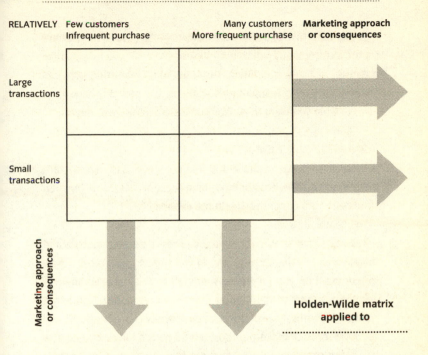

RELATIVELY | Few customers
Infrequent purchase | Many customers
More frequent purchase | **Marketing approach or consequences**

Large transactions

Small transactions

Marketing approach or consequences

Holden-Wilde matrix applied to

owners/directors) and your vision for the company in the near future as well as an understanding of what's realistic given the current trading environment. At this stage there's no point in looking too far ahead; usually two years is fine to start with.

1. **We want to build a business that makes a real difference to the cleanliness of the environment in Yorkshire.**
2. **In the next two years we will grow from a turnover of £200,000 to £350,000.**

It is important that you think of this document as an *action plan*. It's not there to impress anyone with your grasp of business school jargon. The marketing strategy itself is simply every activity that you undertake to achieve the marketing objectives that you have set for your company, which we'll look at shortly. If you're already in business, you almost certainly carry out some marketing activities already; if you're contemplating starting up, you probably have some ideas of what you want to do. You could start with something like:

Your values and purpose

Setting these down in black and white is never easy. For a start, there is always the possibility of being laughed at. Most 'mission statements' are cringe-worthy in the extreme.

You can be different.

Ask yourself what is it about your business that *really* matters and therefore what value or principle do you want to stick most closely to? For example, you might see your staff as a valuable commodity and set out to treat them better than your competitors. You might want to work closely with the local community (see Chapter 6) and set down roots, or make your business stand out for your customers by making *their* lives better. There are as many alternatives as there are small businesses, since each one is different.

What business are you in?

Next, set out a clear statement of the business you are in and, crucially, your insight into that business.

If you've played with the HW matrix and you have some background knowledge of the sector and its prospects for growth, you should be able to say something interesting about your unique take on the industry – or the part of it you are interested in.

We see the opportunity to sell a home collection service to local authorities as they seek to comply with government directives.

34

or

> We will be able to grow (along with the market) at 12%, representing a growth of £24,000 in sales. However, we would aim to add an additional £70,000-worth of business from local authority contracts for more complex sorting of recyclable waste.

As you can see, the opportunities as you describe them can be inspirational because of their 'eureka' quality (no-one else has seen this opportunity) or because of the figures involved.

Your next step will be to detail the actions you are going to take to realise these opportunities – essentially by understanding your customers better than the competition does. At this stage we do not expect you to know *exactly* what you want to achieve. What you should have, however, is a clearer idea of how you see your business, what your business has to do in the next 12–24 months, and some ideas about how you might get there.

What about customers?

You need to have an understanding of the way people consume your products or services. We often talk about the 'level of involvement' of a purchase, or how long it takes us to buy a product. Put simply, the more important a purchase is perceived to be, the more likely it is that the stages referred to are plain to see. For unimportant purchases, the whole decision-making process can be over in the blink of an eye. When you are selling 'impulse' purchases you may, literally, have a couple of seconds to attract the attention of a customer and convince them to act.

We've already suggested that involvement is significant for a small business, since it's implicit in the Holden-Wilde matrix.

Whilst the involvement related to the size of the transaction seems clear enough, the relevance of frequency of purchase is worth thinking about a little more.

When a customer has a regular requirement for a product or service, it's likely she will establish a routine that is convenient. If the product is relatively unimportant then convenience may be paramount. Conversely, there might be a greater 'time cost' in making a buying decision for an infrequent product or service where the customer has to gather quite a lot of new information on an unfamiliar area.

So, in the grid below we have put in brackets what we recommend you think about; is cost more significant than convenience, or is convenience more important than cost? Again, think about this for *your* customers ... and those of your competitors if you can.

RELATIVELY	Few customers Infrequent purchase	Many customers More frequent purchase
Large transactions (from the point of view of the customer)	Higher involvement (cost)	Lower involvement (convenience)
Small transactions (from the point of view of the customer)	Higher involvement (convenience)	Lower involvement (cost)

We should stress, the grid isn't a perfect representation of reality and positions on this grid are relative to each other. As we have seen, the beginning of our planning process is about developing a sense of where we are and where we *could* be. What happens if we imagine our business to be in the bottom right corner and what happens if we move towards the top left? You might find that you have to label the boxes in the model slightly differently as you discover more about *your* customers and *their* relationship with your product. Later, these ideas about position and direction turn into marketing strategy.

For the moment, however, it's enough to ask ourselves questions about how customers make the decisions they do. How involved are they in two senses of the word? Are customers *involved* in the category and is the decision-making process *involved* — that is, lengthy and time consuming? If we don't know, we need to find out.

Real retail experiences

As an example of consumer insight, research carried out into the experiences of shopping revealed some insights into the pleasures of buying in stores which challenge a commonly-held view that shoppers like to interact with other shoppers or staff[2].

The research identifies a group of shoppers who are 'joyless'; those who do not enjoy shopping in a store environment. While this research was carried out on women in the United States, it is likely that there are similar groups of women in the UK who are also dissatisfied with the experience of shopping in stores but, of course, still want to purchase things. For other shoppers there *was* enjoyment to be found and, not surprisingly, the major one was to do with coming away with the feeling that they had 'got a bargain'.

Now, the question for you is, how extensive is the decision-making process *your* customers go through? What happens in each stage? Do you really understand the parts they enjoy and the parts they don't? This is important, because understanding customers better than others is a source of advantage over the competition[3].

At the very least, you should be able to assess the importance of your customers by collecting together some comparatively simple data.

How important are your customers?

You might like to consider how you evaluate your existing customers, asking, for example, what percentage of each customer's requirements you meet (shared pocket or wallet).

Customers

Contribute	% of *your* turnover	% of *your* profit	% of *their* requirements
Daly's	12	15	50
BAe	30	15	5
Askew Engineering	17	32	70
Monitor Retail Systems	4	1	100
Skane Engineering	15	21	10
Rutherford & Co	2	6	30
Lucas	20	10	1

How would you go about discovering this information for your company? How would you quantify their 'requirements' in order to quantify your 'share'? What difference would the definition of those requirements make? To what use could you put this information?

Some of this data might be available through your sales or accounting software. Finding out what percentage of your customers' requirements you fill might be information that is gleaned by sales staff or as a result of carrying out research. We will look at this in more detail in Chapter 3.

In the table above, if we consider Lucas, here is a company that gives you 20% of your business, being therefore your third biggest customer, and yielding a fair profit at 10%, but you only account for 1% of its business. You might be vulnerable to losing this business if your product or service isn't differentiated. Lucas might decide to streamline the number of suppliers its uses and you could end up a casualty of this process. You might view BAe in the same way as Lucas. Perhaps you should be looking at ways of imposing further barriers to the competitors who are keen to take over this business. Can you look at our service levels and improve upon them?

Experience tells us that not enough companies have even this level of information, which in itself makes them more vulnerable.

What next?

As these first two chapters have shown, customers are the focus of your company – as they should be for every business. All we are suggesting here is that you simply try to find out more about them than you know at present.

Whoever your customers are (companies or individuals), compile a database of your customers and fill in the gaps with the information you already have. The less you are able to fill in immediately, the more you will need to find out. Don't make up answers, don't make excuses, but *do* recognise the need to fill in these gaps – and then keep the information up to date.

Try to work out your customers' contribution to profit and set up the columns we suggested to estimate what percentage of *their* needs you are responsible for. These are only exercises in estimating the value of customers, but it's important you know.

Notes/References

1. Christmas 2005 retail trading analysis.
2. Cox, A., et al (2005). 'Reassessing the pleasures of store shopping. *Journal of Business Research*, No. 58, pp. 250–259.
3. To be precise, we think it's the only competitive advantage as far as marketing is concerned.

3 FINDING OUT ABOUT CUSTOMERS

This chapter will help you to find the most cost-effective ways of collecting what is, for many, the lifeblood of the business: information – more specifically, customer and market information. You will find ways of tracking down the data you need for the planning areas we have introduced in the first two chapters. For those of you already in business, your findings might encourage you to rethink your existing strategy.

Where are all the customers?

One of the biggest problems you'll have with accepting market research as a key marketing tool will be your perception of it. It usually conjures up images of interviewers stopping people in the high street and asking them questions about their choice of cat food – or, alternatively, of the hundreds of surveys offered by websites and television programmes that ask us to answer yes or no to complex issues. In their defence, both these types of research do important work, but they form only a small part of what market research has to offer your business.

Perhaps what we need to point out at this stage is that research into small business failure has often revealed that a major cause is a lack of understanding of a market and its customers. If you don't really know your customers, how can you serve them?

We see a particular type of business appear on our high streets every year. We refer to it as the 'coffee/card shop fantasy'. This is the coffee shop that opens on the high street with a selection of (usually very artistic) cards on offer, and then closes down about nine months later[1]. If you follow this chapter carefully, we could be saving you some heartache, as well as a considerable amount of your (or the bank's) money!

Aren't good business ideas based on hunches?

It's far too easy to rely on hunches* when setting up a new business, and there are plenty of examples of people who have been successful without resorting to market research. Unfortunately, there are many more who have lost significant sums of money investing in businesses that were destined to fail. While spending £5,000 pounds on market research might seem a poor investment to many small business owners, it might ultimately save you the £60,000 that you lose when your business fails. Don't worry, we aren't suggesting that you spend £5,000. In fact, many of the techniques that we will show you will cost considerably less. And as they say about education too: if you think such knowledge is expensive, you should try ignorance.

* Indeed some rely on lunches. Why is it that business ideas sound so good over a restaurant meal with a couple of drinks and a sympathetic friend? It's usually because you have an uncritical audience. However, it's the friends who tell you the unvarnished truth who are truly invaluable.

Somebody has already done some of your research for you!

Tracking down data that is already published (secondary data) is referred to as 'desk research'. From our experience of working with small business managers, desk research is very often a neglected area. Most people are unaware of the range of publications available to buy or even access in a local or central library. Off-the-shelf market research data is a very useful starting point and is available for most key markets. Even for brand new product or service ideas, simply accessing data on population trends and indicators of social groups may be an important starting point. Even if the data isn't bang up to date, it's better than no data at all.

Getting started

There are a number of questions that you need to answer before you consider investing your money – or anybody else's, for that matter – in a new business venture. Your first port of call should be the publications which are either free to access in libraries or online, or which are available for a subscription or purchase. The more popular the business concept, such as retail or a restaurant, the more likely you are to be able to find background information. In some industries, this includes a complete breakdown of a market, including the key competitors and some details on the customers. Incidentally, if a publication is not in your local library, ask the librarian to get it for you. It may be free to do so or cost a few pounds for information that has cost thousands of pounds to compile – that is definitely shoestring territory!

Which is the most effective technique to use?

There isn't necessarily a 'best way' of doing market research. Your own research (for so-called 'primary' data) could be surveys, face-to-face or phone interviews, focus groups, or ask people to sample your new products or services. The simple answer is that there isn't usually one technique to suit all businesses, so be prepared to try a mix of techniques[2].

Perception isn't reality

When you're researching a new market, you need to find out what's *really* happening, rather than what you *think* might be happening. Don't make assumptions when you're calculating the size of your potential market. Perhaps we can test you? Do most people go on holiday every year? Does everybody eat out? Do all men play football on a regular basis? Does everyone drink soft fizzy drinks? Do all young people go to night-clubs?

Do you know the answers? Perhaps you'll be shocked to hear that around 40% of the population never go on holiday from one year to the next. Most men don't play football regularly; in fact the vast majority of males are 'football disinterested' and virtually never watch a game live or on television. These figures can make a difference. If there are 20,000 18- to 24-year-olds in your area, and only 50% are likely to have any interest in your new business, then this is a much smaller potential market than if say 80% are likely to consume. Crucially, this group might also not be big enough to sustain your business.

Making the most of publications

You need to learn some of the lessons from the people who work in marketing, and who make regular use of affordable published data. One such book is *The Marketing Pocket Book*[3]. Costing less than £40, this annual publication contains useful market research data from which to start – information about population sizes, regional breakdowns, advertising coverage, consumption trends, as well as some market research data about key markets.

To illustrate how spending can save you money, in one small town, two card shops opened in the high street in the space of six months. Within a year both had gone out of business. *The Marketing Pocket Book* would tell you how much is spent on greetings cards, the average spend per card and the total value of the market. If the owners of the card shops had used this basic information along with simple research techniques (like knowing the population of the town), then neither would have opened!

Government data (published for the Office of National Statistics) is another useful source, much of which is available online[4]. Market researchers will also use these types of guide to gain some insight into a new research project. While this type of publication does not answer all of your research questions, it can set the boundaries of your own research. For example, by referring to national statistics, you can select towns over a certain size or calculate the percentage of a local population that is retired or has children living at home.

More basic, free information can be found online through such websites as LoveMyTown (*www.lovemytown.co.uk*) and UpMyStreet (*www.upmystreet.com*) but you will have to put some time into exploring these. UpMyStreet, for example, can give you useful comparisons between cities, towns and areas for such things as house prices or the number of chemists' shops. Funnily enough, UpMyStreet can also tell you how many greetings cards shops there are in a town.

For a few pounds more

There are more specialist publications which you should consider. These are market and industry reports produced by organisations such as Mintel or Keynote[5] and they deal more comprehensively with certain market categories, ranging from the hairdressing market to personal training and leisure.

There is so much information in this type of publication alone that they should be compulsory reading for any new restaurant owner, shopkeeper or anyone looking to set up a business in the leisure industry. They consider trends and very often carry out attitude surveys of consumers. If your customers are companies, you might be surprised at the number of specialist surveys that can also be found, ranging from electrical manufacturing equipment to pet supplies. While such publications might easily start at £300, some are carried in business libraries and are therefore freely available for reference. However, even at £300, they will represent an important investment in your business and give you information your rivals may not have.

You only have to reach your break-even target

In developing your business plan, which you started in Chapter 2, bear in mind the minimum amount of business you need (remember your corporate objectives, survive, stabalise or grow) in order to survive, or your 'break-even figure', in terms of the number of customers you need. This can be based, if need be, on an average spend for the industry, but obviously real figures from your own trading will be preferable (as you might get from the exercise on page 38). These figures give a baseline – an acid test – for your research. If the market you explore doesn't yield this, you can't succeed.

For example, if you run a printing business with an average order amount of £100 and you need to take £1,000 to break even, you need an average of 10 customers per week. If you already have two regular customers who will spend £400 per week between them, you'll need another two average customers at £100 per order.

Unfortunately at this stage of the calculations, many budding entrepreneurs launch their business without any further research, their confidence boosted by what they see as an easy target. If you need to find 50 customers per week, ask yourself where those customers are, and how big a pool of customers will you need to hit that weekly target? You'll then need to do a bit more research. The 'Market Breakdown Calculator' which we introduce later is a useful tool.

Working out the size of the market

Your market may, of course, be rather more difficult to define. We will look at a way of trying to calculate its size. This technique can be used to try and predict the outcome of targeting specific market segments with new products or services. So, for example, if one of the target groups for your new beauty salon is women aged between 35 and 44 who need to get away from their families once a month, then you should be able to calculate the likely size of this group. You might estimate that they account for 30% of all women in this age group. Remember though that your research will need to find out what is a realistic target for your business. It doesn't matter too much if the real figure is 20% or even 40%; the most important thing is that you don't develop your marketing plan based on the assumption that they account for 80% of this group or that they all will buy every week, and to check back with your break-even figures. If you start with the people in your own town, for example, you could then do separate calculations for people in neighbouring towns.

What about my new restaurant?

Many people dream of setting up a new restaurant, but the failure rate of new restaurants has probably created a thriving market for the sale of second-hand restaurant furniture! Having said that, there has been some growth among child-friendly food outlets. Anyone with small children will know how difficult it can be to take them out for a meal. Some fast food restaurants and out-of-town pub-style restaurants spotted the opportunity though, and began to offer in-house play areas and a range of food and drink for children. A visit to a 'Charlie Chalk' restaurant became an important family visit, working out at about £6 per head, as opposed to the £3 per head for a child's meal at a fast food restaurant. How times have changed: parents are now more aware of the dangers of processed food and a growing number are moving away from fast food outlets. In Sevenoaks in Kent, a town with a very large middle-class population, McDonald's has recently closed down its restaurant. There is clearly an opportunity for a restaurant to incorporate the entertainment elements of its competitors and serve home-made, nutritious and fun food for children at affordable prices. How can you use desk research to help you measure the potential market, and then use your own preliminary research to test your concept?

Using the Market Breakdown Calculator[6]

On the next two pages we introduce a technique that helps you to calculate the likely market value and volume of specific customer groups that you would like to target. The starting point is always the total population of a given area; by introducing different variables you can reduce this figure to a more realistic target. On the whole its safer to underestimate the market.

The information that you need to feed into the calculator is from secondary published research and also from your primary research. You carry out separate calculations for each identified group of

Variable	% value	Population	Source of information	Secondary sources of information
Population of Easytown	100%	25,000	Population trends	
Married people 20–45	50%*	12,500	National statistics	
Married people 20–45 with children	80%	10,000	National statistics	
Married people 20–45 with children who eat out as a family once a week	70%	7,000	Local statistics	

Variable	% value	Population	Source of information
			Primary sources of information
Prefer children's entertainment as part of the package	80%	5,600	Market research survey
Expressed an interest in a new type of family restaurant	60%	3,360	Consumer testing results
Those who will actually purchase when given the option	40%	1,344	Company experience of those that will actually purchase
Those who will continue to purchase after an initial period of one month	40%	538	Forecast based on experience of introducing new products
Average number of visits per week	0.5 visits	269	Estimated number of visits per week
Average price paid per family visit £50		£13,450	Initial estimate of business per week

* Multiply this figure by the population figure in the row above.

potential customers. If you set this information up in a computer spreadsheet, you will be able to make adjustments to the overall figures.

So, say that your first target group is Easytown residents, married with children and aged 20–45, who eat out as a family at least once a week, and who choose a restaurant which caters for the entertainment needs of their children. You then use your own research or primary research to reduce the starting figures to a more realistic total.

What you will show is that the total amount of business for this sector is about £13,450 per week – that's the figure for all restaurants of this kind in the area. If you need to take, say, £2,000 per week, then you are looking to take about a 15% share of this sector. You haven't calculated the competition, but if you have these figures then you can factor them into the equation.

You could pop into a local restaurant each lunchtime and evening for a week to see how many people are there. Armed with the menu you could 'guestimate' their average expenditure. What 'share' do they have?

Hold on! We can almost hear the clatter of books being cast aside as many of you rush to set up this new type of restaurant and the top line of your business plan looks very healthy indeed. Well, this is just a starting point and the figures might well be realistic. They do, however, need some fine tuning and you need to work out the size of some of the other segments that you could target. You would also need to take a more pessimistic view. The value of this system is that you can add in new data and make adjustments quite easily on your spreadsheet. In some cases, the figures do not make for a very attractive proposition, and this might cause you to be slightly more cautious. This is not a bad thing – you are, after all, trying to reduce the risk of failure.

Using this technique, you can now look at the other market segments you want to measure. More importantly, you can make some revisions to your main segment. Imagine that you revise your estimates down by 10%. Can you still operate at these figures? If yes, your new venture is likely to pose less risk. These figures can also be used to set daily and weekly sales targets, and will enable you to set up an early-warning system if you don't hit your targets.

Then you can extend this technique to help you develop your monthly targets, taking into account the seasonal factors which affect your businesses either positively or adversely.

Don't use market research as a sales technique!

The Market Research Industry is regulated by the Market Research Society (MRS), which has very strict guidelines on the use of market research techniques. We don't want you turn into 'suggers', or people who sell under the guise of conducting market research. Usually a few questions at the beginning give you the impression that your opinion is important, but then comes the sales pitch. This practice is off-putting and will make people less likely to respond to genuine questioning. It's a shame, as our experience of carrying out research shows that when people are approached in the right way and at the right time, they are very willing to share their experiences as customers and often help to identify opportunities or weaknesses in the market.

What about using an independent researcher?

Using an independent researcher to carry out your research needs is another option, but it is a pricey one: the cost is likely to start at around £1,000. It's even more expensive for specialist B2B markets than for consumer markets. You need to weigh up the pros and cons of this approach. Is it better to spend £10,000 on research and find out that your business will struggle, or spend £100,000 on setting the business up *without* research … and then see it go under after a just a few months? This is perhaps the worst part about small business consulting. Small business failure leaves casualties, unfortunately, and it's never pleasant to see people lose savings, redundancy and inheritance money on failed businesses.

Sampling is important

Before you start your survey, you need to get to grips with the concept of sampling. To understand a group of consumers or potential consumers, you don't need to interview every single one of them to find out their views or opinions. If you choose your subjects carefully, it's likely that their thoughts can be taken as representative of others within the group. As many market research professionals will tell you, you only need to eat a sample of the whole cake to know what it tastes like! Indeed the opinion polls run by organisations such as MORI demonstrate this perfectly.

It is possible to interview a sample of only about 2,000 people and for the results to be representative of the voting population of the whole country, and for the results to be accurate with a reasonable margin of error. Of course you do not need to interview 2,000 people, but you can endeavour to make your sample as representative as possible. Having said that, sampling does not mean that you only ask the people you intend to sell to. That would be like David Cameron only polling Conservative voters to see if he could win the election.

If you are setting out to test whether your product will appeal to, say, 'young adults', then you might need to research it with a slightly broader range of ages – 16–30 perhaps. Their responses may tell you more precisely which age group to aim at. Since there are very few completely new products and services, you are also likely to be trying to find out what *kind* of young people your product appeals to and this may involve questions about their occupations, income, other purchases or hobbies and interests.

Sampling for business to business markets

If your customers are other companies, you will need to consider their (potential) value to you as customers as another variable to be researched. It's best not to use the same sampling technique as we recommend for consumer markets. If there are 50 businesses in your market but three account for 40% of the total turnover of the industry, it would be very important for you to interview all three before then sampling the next 'layer' of companies that account for the remaining 60% of the total market.

Questions, questions and more questions

For many, the questionnaire *is* market research and it is probably the most frequently used tool of them all. But you need to understand the advantages and disadvantages of the questionnaire. Some basic principles need to be followed if you are to get the best from them.

The first problem that an inexperienced researcher encounters is how many questions to include? And the answer is always, 'it depends what you want to find out'. Be careful of asking questions that push the respondent into answering in a certain way. Loaded questions produce pretty meaningless results, and making respondents feel uncomfortable might also lead to them giving you the answer that they think that you want. Remember, you want to capture the truth and your style of questioning may determine how successful your questionnaire will be.

It is almost universally the case that, before you carry out any kind of measurement research (known as 'quantitative'), you should carry out some exploratory ('qualitative') research first. You might need to carry out some interviews, focus groups or observation (like the restaurant visits on p. 50) in order to gain a better understanding of the type of people you're going to survey, and exactly how you should construct the questionnaire. You need to ask questions in a language that the customers will understand and give them choices that mean something to them.

If you think that compiling questions to gauge people's attitude towards a particular product is common sense, then consider the following options. Do you ask people for their attitude about the product, or do you compile a list of attitudes typical of consumers of this type of product, and ask respondents to reply using a scale of 1 to 5, or strongly agree, agree, neither, disagree or strongly disagree? For example:

What do you think about the car valeting service? Please write in the space below.

....

....

or

Please tick the statement that best reflects your view of our valeting service.

- **It's an excellent service**
- **The service is efficient**
- **The service is acceptable, but not great?**   ✓
- **The service is disappointing**

■ **The service is poor**
■ **Other (please specify)**

or

Please indicate below how far these statements reflect
your own views:

	Disagree strongly	Disagree	Neither agree nor disagree	Agree	Agree strongly
I enjoy having the car clean inside				✓	
I am always disappointed by the standard of cleaning	✓				
When I pick up my car after cleaning, it feels like new	✓				

and so on . . .

Any of the above may produce some useful information, but all of
them might miss out on something fundamental to the customer's

experience of your product or service. Before you even know what to ask, you have to know something about the customer's attitudes, values, beliefs, knowledge and behaviour.

So, talking to customers at any time to get a feel for how they talk, whether indeed they ever think about your product ('Oh, I didn't know you valeted the car when you serviced it!'), what prompted them to come to you in the first place and so on is always valuable. It's research you can do every day you're in business. Just make sure you record it. See Chapter 7 for help on how to do that.

Choose your researchers carefully

A word of caution about how you choose your researchers. The people who actually ask the questions of consumers can influence the likely responses. Young people, for example, will be reluctant to tell the truth about their consumption of certain products if the researcher is roughly the same age as their parents or guardians.

Should we use online surveys?

There are a number of websites offering online surveys which also analyse the data captured. This is a wonderful development for market researchers, but approach them with some caution. Stick by the principles of sampling and make sure that the completed surveys are from a representative group of people. It might be good to get feedback from 300 people, but if you don't know exactly who they represent, the data might be misleading. Websites such as Survey Monkey (*www.surveymonkey.com*) and SySurvey (*www.sysurvey.com*) offer a fairly comprehensive service for online research, but you may find that the prices are rather more than 'shoestring'. You can, of course, construct surveys using such facilities as Yahoo or Google groups – basic word-processed questionnaires can be distributed. If you're a competent user, you can even construct forms to be completed electronically. Incidentally, online communities like Facebook and Google Groups and others are valuable places to chat to customers and users of products. SySurvey and others also enable the management of online focus groups.

Interviews

Simply phoning up and asking to meet a potential customer is the most direct way of finding out information about your competitors. You'll get turned down more often than not, but it's still worth a try. We are no longer amazed at how willing people are to speak about their suppliers. Many are quite happy to discuss their working relationships and the findings can be revealing. If they are unhappy with their suppliers, they're almost certainly going to tell you about it. This type of information is vital and can well present the opportunity to move your business idea further. Surely you are not going to make the same mistakes as your competitor?

In order to take advantage of these opportunities, always prepare exactly what you would like to ask in an interview. Remember that you might only get one opportunity and need to make best use of your interviewees' time. Remember also that you might be working in the same industry as the people you are interviewing, so try to create a lasting (good!) impression.

Observation

Doesn't it make sense to observe businesses and look at how their customers or potential customers behave? As a former colleague would always say to his clients, just imagine how much you can find out about people simply by looking at the way they shop. Several retail groups still carry out observational research when trying to find the location for their next outlet. Their formulae are a closely guarded secret, but not difficult to replicate. By calculating the total 'foot traffic' – the total number of people who walk past the shop – they can estimate how many of those are likely to be their customers. No doubt they base this on the actual foot traffic at their existing venues and compare this to the actual number of customers who enter their shops on a weekly basis. One leading UK retailer used automatic counters at the doors of its shops to measure how many people came in during opening hours. Again this is valuable information when analysing sales; it's not hard to calculate the total number of sales divided by the total number of people who appear to have come into the shop.

Mystery shopping

The aim of mystery shopping is for a researcher to enter a business in the guise of a potential customer to see at first hand how sales assistants and other employees deal with customers, particularly when they think that managers aren't present. This technique is a great way of finding out how customer-focused staff are, and can highlight significant weaknesses in a business. Be careful how you use this technique (it's far easier online or by phone) because if the staff realise that there is a mystery shopper about, they're likely to put on a fine performance. If used correctly, though, mystery shopping is an extremely useful research tool.

Focus groups

If you're thinking about using focus groups, approach with care. Focus groups should be used primarily to test the views of customers, potential customers and your competitors. They are purely exploratory and should give you some insight into the buying decisions that people make. The sessions are managed by a researcher who attempts to record all of the information from the session. There should be an incentive for people to take part – after all, you are asking for an hour of their time – and the groups are usually made up of six to eight people, but they can contain as few as four.

If you are running it yourself, you'll need:

- **a room (without distractions)**
- **comfortable chairs**
- **refreshments**
- **tape or digital recorder**
- **pad for taking notes**
- **topic guide (your plan!)**
- **props (if you are introducing a new product or concept about which you need some comments)**
- **payment or reward for those taking part**

The main pitfall of focus groups is that they're not usually statistically representative of any larger population. It's also easy for the inexperienced researcher to lose control of the discussion and let individuals dominate the group, which means missing out on answers to vital questions. In skilled hands, though, the focus group can give you invaluable new leads, especially when completely unexpected ideas arise. For example, in a project we undertook for a new radio franchise, our discussion groups introduced us to 'sports haters'; people who cannot bear to listen to sport reports on the radio. We subsequently tested this concept in our survey of 600 listeners, and found that this was a very significant group and recommended it be considered when planning programming on the radio station.

Avoid using family and friends as part of the group, a common mistake of the novice researcher. While they might provide some insight, they are likely to only confirm what you wanted to hear, rather than express the views of typical consumers! Remember that many new restaurant ideas are started at dinner parties where the guests, who are rightly impressed by your culinary skills, suggest that you should be cooking for a living and making money.

A word about focus groups for business customers

Don't. As we have seen, business-to-business (B2B) markets generally have fewer customers than in a consumer market. It is not advisable to try and set up focus groups for these customers as not only are they likely to be geographically dispersed, but they are also likely to be each others' competitors. You probably would not want key customers together comparing the prices you charge.

Using the Internet

Information is readily available on the Web, and few business disciplines are overlooked. Start by using sites such as Google, Excite, Yahoo and Yell in which you can search other sites or browse categories of industry rather like a directory. There are plenty of industry-specific sites or even industry-specific journals online too. If you're relatively new to using the Internet, you might want to seek some practical help through short courses provided at local training centres and colleges, but whatever else you do, use the Web and get familiar with it.

As an example, consider the following task. You need to identify the firms in your county that use valves in their production process.

You can start by looking for an industry-specific website; even just using the search term 'valves' in Google throws up thousands of sites. On the first page are firms that supply valves and the various industries they serve. If you explore this, there are likely to be firms featured that you can investigate. An industry-specific site (say for the petrochemical industry – another search) might also link to industry bodies and even a list of members. By searching for an industry-specific journal, you'll very quickly find the journal's website and there will be details of how to get a sample copy. Some publishers might even have a copy for you to download, and so far you haven't needed to leave your desk.

A growing number of people use the Internet as their main search technique. This will also include customers, or in your case, some of your potential customers. As a 'mystery surfer', visit a few of your competitors' websites to see what kind of experience customers are presented with. Some companies still use a basic website that offers very little information and out-of-date links and contact details. If you can identify any weaknesses in your industry, then this might present an opportunity for you. One of our clients developed innovative software which was used to manage sports clubs. While there were several important players in the market, none had managed to offer an online booking system, yet it was requested repeatedly by several potential customers. It's now in place.

What next?

Investment in market research is rarely wasted. It's time for the detective work to begin. Compile a comprehensive list of what you need to know and then set out to try and find that information, using published sources of information, either online or in print. Remember to look for the nearest libraries that will allow you access to industry reports. Much of the most valuable information will probably need to be paid for, and you will find many websites that offer information but may require you to subscribe before you can get your hands on it. Don't give up straight away, but spend time looking for other websites where the report isn't password protected. It doesn't always work but it's worth a try. In the end you may need to pay, but it may be a good investment.

There may be somebody else who is better than you at tracking down research data within an organisation, so spread the job around. Having read the previous chapters of this book, you'll still have gaps in your knowledge to fill in. Don't be tempted to skip this section and move on to the next chapters; keep working on your research and you'll be surprised how much you can find out in a short period of time. Once you have this data, you will be in a more informed position to make strategic decisions. But you should expect to have to keep coming back to this chapter to search out answers to the questions that will arise as your plans develop. Remember want we said; it is better to find out that your plan is flawed *before* you launch than four weeks into the new business!

Notes/ References

1. Just before this book went to press, the very 'coffee/card' shop we had in mind as we wrote this, closed down.

2. There is a lot of information at the website run by Research Portals Ltd (*www. marketresearchworld.net*), not only on published research but also on research professionals who may be able to help you.

3. *The Marketing Pocket Book 2009*, World Advertising Research Centre (WARC), *www.warc.com*. Other publications are *European Marketing Pocket Book* and *Americas Pocket Book*. For summary information go to BDO's website, *www. bdo.uk.com* and download their Consumer Pocketbook.

4. *www.statistics.gov.uk*

5. Mintel Market Intelligence Reports (*www.mintel.com*). A typical report is the *Air Conditioning, Industrial Report*, UK, August 2006 at a cost of £550. Keynote Publications (*www.keynote.co.uk*), has over 1,000 reports available to purchase online. A typical report is *Fast Food and Home Delivery Outlets*, 2006.

6. This 'breakdown' process is explored in a book now in its 11th edition and still one of the best for the academic study of small business (Moore, C. W., Petty, J. and Longenecker, J. G. (2005). *Small Business Management*, South-Western Publishing Co, USA). It's complementary to the more conventional 'build-up' method used when a small business starts with the customers it knows and finds similar customers in order to estimate total demand. Sadly, small businesses tend to ignore the 'reality check' given by market breakdown.

4 THE BEGINNINGS OF STRATEGY

In this chapter we have . . . the bigger picture! Everything that you've discovered about yourself, your company and your customers is now put to use and you will develop a range of alternative marketing strategies that address different customers or groups of customers.

You will select one or more clearly defined strategies for your business and begin to see how it can be implemented. As you progress, you should become more and more certain of the direction of your business – based on your understanding of your customers.

Reality check

The first part of this book has dealt with all of the areas that *everyone* needs to understand about marketing. However this is where the action starts and we (that is, you) start to look at the decisions you should consider making. Then you make them.

Remember, as we discussed briefly in Chapter 1, you only have three possible corporate objectives:

1. **survive**
2. **stabilise**
3. **grow**

Of course almost every business would hope to do all three. But depending on your position at the moment, you might have to concentrate on item 1 before you move on to 2 or 3.

If you have followed the guidelines we suggested, particularly as you consider your current position and where you want your business to go, then it should be fairly clear which of these is your main concern. Ideally, you should also be able to put some figures to this. If you've looked at how many actual customers there are, your capacity and your ability to attract and service them, you should be able to write down a figure that tells you how many sales you must make and what value they must have – in total and on average.

You have to be able to produce the quantifiable objectives that your company needs to achieve in order to carry on in business! In a retail situation, you could set your objective as receiving 300 visits per week with an average spend of £15 per person. An engineering company might look to increase sales by 5% per week or per month.

If you have used the Holden-Wilde matrix, you might also have a good idea of how you might achieve such objectives. Remember, the model is there to help you create some space in your marketplace for movement. When you begin to see the direction in which you have to go, you have the beginnings of a strategy which involves long-term and important changes.

What do strategies look like?

The real answer is that there is no single correct way to codify a strategy for your company. However, there are numerous wrong ways. And we use the word 'codify' deliberately instead of 'write' because some of the best strategies for small businesses are never written down[1]. Actually, we think you *should* have a go at writing it down, but don't get bogged down with writing it like an essay or a formal business plan. Most importantly, share it around those people who have to make it happen. Incidentally, there's no reason why it has to be on neatly typed A4 sheets of paper, in a folder. Why not write it on poster-sized sheets and pin it to the wall for everyone to see?

A good strategy summarises where your company is now (and this can and should include figures), then describe where you want to get to. It should then explain how you are going to get there, by doing things *with, for* or *to* customers.

Here's an example of how one company sets the scene for its strategy:

> We currently serve 120 customers annually, cleaning office and factory space ranging from 230m2 to 3,030m^2 and our contracts range in value from £2,000 to £9,500 per annum. We have identified three kinds of customer, each of which delivers a different profit margin.

1. **Small office, low skill – 17% gross profit**
2. **Large office, low skill + security issue – 22% gross profit**
3. **Factory/workshop, high skill + health and safety issue – 16% gross profit**

> The number of contracts, the total contract value and the profit for these customers groups are given below . . .

Sometimes it's useful shorthand to develop names for these groups of customers, but beware; nicknames that are less than complimentary have a habit of sneaking out and getting back to the customers you serve. No-one wants to know they are a 'low-value' customer or, worse still, that they are categorised as 'difficult'.

At this stage, you have a pretty concise picture of where you are.

But having read Chapter 3, you can now fill this out to estimate the amount of growth available to you, both within your existing customer-base and in the market. Of course you may have more or less confidence in the figures from your research, so you might like to develop several versions of your figures – a conservative one, an optimistic one and a 'most likely'. These sorts of 'scenarios' are at least a feature of big business planning.

Again, our cleaning company might prepare something like this:

The tables below show our estimates of the importance of each of these customer groups.

Group 1: Percentage of existing customers' needs met by us
    Estimated value of unmet needs
    Number of similar companies within the borough
    Therefore % served
    Estimate of value of the un-served market
Group 2: ...

As you draft these important first steps in your strategy, be prepared to revise your estimates up and down when better figures come your way. You'll also have to revise your groupings as you often realise that within each group there can be significant variations. As you become more certain about your current position, however, you'll also begin to see directions in which you might move. The likelihood is that you will be pulled in several directions because you want to serve two or more customer groups, each with different needs.

Broadly speaking, you will be developing strategies that show how you are moving in one or other direction around the Holden-Wilde matrix and you can fill this in with as much detail as you need.

RELATIVELY	Few customers Infrequent purchase	Many customer More frequent purchase
Large transactions (from the point of view of the customer)	**1** There are few customers who buy what we make and they generally spend a lot. They're highly involved.	**2** There are many customers (and therefore competitors) and the product is still expensive. They're less involved because it's pretty accessible.
Small transactions (from the point of view of the customer)	**3** This is an infrequent purchase, but people don't see it as high value. However they're involved because it's not routine.	**4** A lot of people buy this frequently and it's not valued highly. They're not involved because it's routine.

Sector 1

In this sector, the key customers are probably relatively easy to locate. However, as there are fewer of them (and you only have a few of those available), you'll have to make sure that you look after them. You need to be absolutely sure of making them come back to you when they next purchase your products or services. If you are trying to grow, are there many more of this type of customer out there?

You also know that the decisions to buy your products/services are more complex, usually involving more than one person. There is a DMU (Decision Making Unit) within these organisations, so ensure you understand the role played by each person in the DMU.

Sector 2

In this segment, the transactions are more frequent but still *relatively* large (from the point of view of the customer). As a result, there's often a high level of competition. Again, it's useful to understand who is taking part in decision making since such purchases still often represent complex decisions.

Good examples of this type of market are estate agents, car dealerships, electricians and suppliers of 'business process' products, or components for other businesses such as builders' merchants or automotive parts suppliers.

There are many companies in this sector of the grid and your strategic options are less clear-cut. They require a more considered approach. You won't be able to satisfy the whole market, so you need to select carefully. Do some of your customers appear to have characteristics of the other sectors? Can you find ways of appealing to those that produce greater profit? Can you, in effect, pick off a cluster of customers who are towards quadrant 1?

You might be able to 'reframe' the marketplace so that you ignore some customers and some competitors and concentrate on others. Sorry, but then you may have to fill out another Holden-Wilde matrix with new information. It's all part of considering strategic alternatives.

Another important consideration is that there may still be relatively high levels of emotional involvement in the decision – especially when the customer is an individual – so you should be exploring the value of branding your organisation. Customers have choice and just because there appears to be less involvement than for those further left (on the grid), it doesn't mean there isn't *any*. Apply some common sense too.

One strategic option is to understand the way customers 'cluster' in the market by the benefits they value, and then see how closely what you offer suits the different segments in the marketplace. It might be that you have particular expertise in key segments and could reinforce the barriers to competitive approaches to your customers. These clusters or segments can also be spread around the Holden-Wilde matrix. So, for example, if we apply the matrix only to estate agencies then professional landlords and property developers are in a different space to individual first-time buyers.

Sector 3

Here we are dealing with smaller transactions and infrequent purchases. This is a difficult sector in which to build up loyalty and one where there are frequent complaints about poor customer service. In fact if your business relies heavily, or entirely, on this segment you should probably consider shifting it towards another segment. Can you specialise to attract a smaller, but more profitable customer? Can you give a sometimes 'hidden' service a high-street presence?

Good examples of businesses in this category are restaurants, chimney sweeps and hair salons. Experienced hair salon managers often say that new customers are unlikely to become loyal unless you get them to come back on at least four occasions. There are just too many competitors for customers to try out. Considering the amount of money spent trying to recruit new customers, perhaps more should be done to encourage repeat purchase. This might involve setting up a customer relationship management system to help manage the appointment system (see Chapter 6).

FRESHLY COOKED GOURMET TREATS YOUR DOG WILL LOVE

One of our favourite examples is the Dog Deli, based in Edinburgh but with a nationwide ambition. It's a very small company with a clear vision of what it is.

Gourmet food for dogs is not a huge market and so there are relatively few customers (compared to the for, market say, Pedigree Pet Foods) spread across the country.

By attending dog shows and country fairs the owners gain access to the *relatively* few customers they need. They can then promote their tasty lamb's liver and organic carrot muffin (tasty, that is, for dogs) and other treats in good-quality paper bags with a simple printed label sealing it.

The positioning is good, their recruitment of their identified market is good. But we wonder if they really make an effort to keep these new customers, who buy once at a country fair but may not visit the website . . .

Sector 4

Here, purchases are more routine and tend to be fairly frequent, almost like commodities. It is likely that a number of customers do not have any commitment to any particular supplier and share their custom around. Good examples of products or services in this sector are newspapers, photocopying paper and confectionery. It can be difficult to change the patterns of behaviour of consumers in this segment, and the purchase might simply be a routine one. This will require exceptional added value to win over new customers or increase the loyalty of existing customers. More than anything else, you must be in the right position at the right time or you have to give people extraordinary reasons to find you.

Again, 'reframing' the marketplace may help. For example, confectionery stores that sell traditional, old-fashioned sweets are springing up on the high street and online. Although these shops might seem to be in competition with the confectionery/ tobacconist/ newsagents 'corner shop', they are actually aiming at a higher-value, less frequent purchase. We wonder if they realise it?

Whatever business you are in, you can map it on the Holden-Wilde matrix at different levels of magnification. Look at the industry as a whole and position yourself. Now, on a clean grid, look at your customers and your closest competitors. Where are you, where are they, where could you be? Look at the ways you could 'reframe' your industry and create space for movement.

Making sense of your strategy

You probably now have a long list of objectives and strategic 'directions' but no clear idea of how you're going to achieve them. If there are too many, which are the most important? These are all a natural result of generating strategic alternatives. But it's good to have a choice and it's often a sign of insufficient preparation when you only have one strategy for the whole company – especially when it makes no mention of customers and their diversity.

In order to make progress, you now need to compare these alternatives with each other.

- **Which offer the best chance of meeting your overall corporate objectives?**
- **Which offer the best growth, the best profit, the most stable business?**
- **Which appear to have less competition?**

Again, comparing these directions on the Holden-Wilde matrix, you can gauge which offers you the strongest position.

Write and re-write your objectives

You need to produce your *quantifiable* objectives. Another way to look at them is to consider them as targets. Having now positioned yourself on the Holden-Wilde grid, it's time to work out some *marketing* objectives. To get you started, here are some examples for different businesses. They each make reference to a particular kind of customer and quantify the target.

Our objective is to gain 10 extra customers who will buy at least £4,000 worth of garments from us each season.

Our objective is to increase the number of evening diners on weekdays from 12 to 24.

Our objective for 'Gold' account customers is to increase the value of their business by 7%.

It's important that you don't consider these to be set in stone – yet. One of the reasons for this flexibility is that, as you write them down, doubts and questions will come to mind and you will inevitably find yourself going off to check this fact or that figure.

If you're lucky, you'll have a business partner to give another opinion on the degree of reality in your objectives! We often hear people telling us that they are going to double their turnover in a year in a market that is only growing by 5%.

At the same time, you will also inevitably find yourself having great ideas about how you can make all this happen. These may be true inspiration, or they may be the dangerous ramblings of an overworked mind. Nevertheless, write them down.

These *are* strategies. There is no more mystery to the word than that. They are possible ways of achieving these important things (your objectives) for your company. What activities could help you to reach these goals? Again, these must be within the capabilities of your organisation and clearly attainable. If you are going to encourage your staff to buy into them, they have to be realistic. If you set out to increase your referrals by X% by spending £Y, what is the impact likely to be? And also, what will you have to do *within* the company to make it happen?

Another important thing will probably happen (if it hasn't already) and that is, you will begin to identify ways you *could* influence your customers' experience of your product or service *if only* you had control over another part of their experience.

For example, a theatrical company using a local authority venue might usually use the bar staff and front of house staff provided by the theatre management, and this would be included in the hire cost. But the theatregoer's experience is strongly influenced by what happens before, during (including the interval) and after the performance itself. Could the producing company gain more by covering these parts of the evening's work themselves? Almost certainly, yes. Being there to greet the audience, especially regulars – maybe even in costume, to point out items of interest in the programmes, to 'talk up' the performance, to convey their own enthusiasm, to ensure that everyone is given the handbill for the next performance and, perhaps the opportunity to buy discounted tickets, would all have enormous benefits for the company. And they may also be able to negotiate the hire cost too.

Seeing all the stages your customers go through and understanding how each contributes to their satisfaction is a valuable addition to thinking about strategy. It's what we've referred to before as the value chain.

Striking a balance

In order fully to understand the choice you have to make between strategies, you need to set down clearly the likely costs and benefits of each one. The costs are often the deciding factor for SMEs, but you should still work through the options. Having a strategy for a significant new market ready and waiting for the right resources might prove useful. For example, in your growing small business you may find that you can't afford to recruit the right skills to make one plan work. The following year, however, when it comes to searching for a new salesperson, you may have a better idea of the kind of person you want.

As you try to assess each of the strategies you have developed, you will begin to wonder what is involved. The costs may not simply be developing a new advert for a local paper.

Strategic alternatives

Remember that these are changes to the *strategy* of the business and its relationship with customers. Strategy, as you will recall, is anything that is of long-term benefit to customers and therefore ultimately to your organisation.

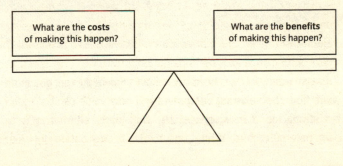

What are the **costs** of making this happen?

What are the **benefits** of making this happen?

Health and safety? Who cares?

The supplier of fire extinguishers to commercial premises is in sector 3 (see pages 68 and 70) because people in offices are not usually aware of the types of fire extinguisher which are available, or how often they need to be replaced.

Further insight would probably show that they are unlikely to admit to this and will be comforted by the fact that the trusty red extinguisher is on view! It might be difficult for sales people to gain entry to these establishments.

If the supplier doesn't realise its current position, this might present an opportunity for another company in sector 4 (see page 71), which already has access to these organisations, perhaps selling more frequent purchases such as stationery. By working on behalf of the fire extinguisher supplier, it could offer an additional service to its customers by checking fire extinguishers in situ, and then advising on options to buy replacements or more appropriate extinguishers.

In our examples, we have seen how somebody can get more value from their existing customers and how value can be added by introducing a new service. The only other alternative is to gain new customers. While this might be an option for your business, we want you to be absolutely clear that this is definitely the riskier option. It is often said that it costs between five and 30 times more to get a new customer than to retain an existing customer, and we don't have any reason to disagree with this statement. In fact our own experience of working with small businesses has shown that it's easy to gobble up the pounds in additional spend on advertising and promotion, forgetting that you've already spent a fortune trying to get your existing customers to engage with you in the first place. Why ignore the investment you've already made in them?

This is why you need to be sure that you are getting as much business as possible from your existing customers *before* looking at the costlier option of new customers. Just think what trying to get new customers involves. You'll have to encourage them to spend less with their existing suppliers, which means breaking down some of the competitive barriers that have been set in place or the habits they have built up. An unknown supplier has to be an awful lot better than an existing supplier to steal customers.

Diversification

Another option you may want to pursue when you're trying to widen your pool of customers is introducing an entirely new product or service for new customers. To be fair, some businesses are able to make this transition very easily, but for others it is a minefield. We also hope you find it strange that we are considering this option, because if you've been following the story so far, you might have worked out why this is the riskiest option of them all. Unfortunately, in our experience this is an option that far too many small businesses pursue. Needless to say the failure rate is very high and it is also likely to have an impact on the existing business.

Not only do you need to design and source a new product or service, you also have to learn about a completely new set of customers. Make no mistake: if you take on this option, you're effectively starting an entirely new business.

Strategic decision making

As you refine your plans you should still be making those notes of the actions that will demonstrate the value of what you are and do to your customers. As your plans become more formal, aim to restate your mission or values, along with your objectives and what you have discovered in your research.

You may end up with a document that looks a bit like this:

Our business: We hand-make and sell beautiful paper.

Our purpose/ what we're best at: Unique and personalised paper with a positive impact on the environment.

Our first year's objectives: £34,000 sales to two customer segments which are. . .

Our second year's objectives: £56,000 sales to the same two customer segments. . .

Our customer insight:

1. **'Green families' want gifts they can feel good about; they like our recycled and natural products because they cut down on waste (especially at Christmas). The products also have a provenance like organic food. Our catalogue (made from our own paper so they can touch and smell) tells that story.**

2. Corporate customers in the creative industries like the clear environmental message combined with the personalisation.

The main reasons customers come back to us:

1. The products change every few months so there's always something new to feel and smell; every sheet of paper and every product is slightly different. Shops don't stock these.

2. We are the only company that can supply obviously recycled paper with logos. We also change the corporate gift range every year so they can be original.

We will increase our existing customers' value:

1. By launching the summer catalogue.

2. By offering more high-value corporate gifts.

We will gain:

1. 120 new 'green family' customers.

2. 20 new corporate customers.

Your plan will contain more detail than this and as you go back through it time and again (yes, it can get dull) you will keep checking for those glaring errors that should be jumping out at you.

A long time ago, before computers ruled the earth . . .

One of our clients was building up a new typesetting and printing company, producing publications for local authorities. He needed to find at least one new customer a year in order to continue growing. One account could easily be worth £200,000 per annum. Unfortunately the barriers to entry were high. Publishers were reluctant to trust a new print company with their magazine with ever-present deadlines.

Our client spotted an opportunity when it became clear that a number of publishers were not taking advantage of new technology. He offered a new potential client a chance to access proofs of his publication online, through a computer provided free of charge. The publisher was able to make observations online and send back suggestions. This reduced the need to courier or fax changes and speeded up communication between the printer and the client.

This was a key turning point and our client won new customers as a result. We have to point out that this was not our idea, but nevertheless a great example of how to convince new customers and 'lock' them in.

One company owner built his plan on recruiting 90 sales consultants in a year. Since six had managed to turn over £90,000, he reasoned that 90 would realise at least £1 million.

Reality bit when it became clear that recruiting the new sales people would turn into (another) full time job[2].

Into action!

So far we've taken a lot of your time trying to get you to understand what marketing actually is rather than what most people think it is. At this point (if you haven't skipped the first half of this book) you should have radically altered your view of your business. You should also have a better understanding of your customers or potential customers.

To recap:

■ **You know that marketing focuses on customers and that everything you do in your company can be measured against its contribution to giving those customers what they want.**

■ **You will also have come to the conclusion that you have to either sell more to your existing customers (in value or volume) or find new customers . . . or both.**

Now all you have to do is make that happen.

Not the 4Ps

Those of you who have read a marketing textbook – even if it was 50 years ago and therefore have (as W. S. Gilbert put it) 'a smattering of elemental strategy' – will know the '4Ps'. We're not going to use them[3]. Instead, we're going to discuss the two categories of things you need to do in order to make your strategy happen. These are not policies or debating points (although you can call them tactics), they are actions.

> ## How about . . .?
>
> . . . buying everyone in your organisation a copy of this book. No, seriously!
>
> Of course we'd like to be at the top of the bestseller list, but the more serious point is the one from Chapter 2. If there are
>
> other important people – well, all people in a small business are important – they too need to understand what you're driving at.
>
> The only way is to have a shared vision of where the company is going and how you're going to get there.
>
> It might help if they read this book too.

Things you can change . . . and things you can't

There is an old saying that there are two things you *shouldn't* worry about: the things you can change and the things you can't. In the first case, you should do something about them and in the second case, don't waste your time.

In the same way, small businesses should focus their attention on the things they *do* control. We've already said that your business can't control the environment or, indeed, the market as a whole (although you must be aware of it and, if necessary, prepared to react quickly). It's one area where small business can out-manoeuvre big business. But customers are **the** priority and you can do a lot to influence them.

In the next couple of chapters we'll give you much more advice on how you can manage customers – both those you have already and those you have yet to attract.

But there is a long list of basic things you need to monitor and get right. They directly affect your customers and, cumulatively, they add up to how you put your strategic ideas into action. These are the elements that meet your customers' needs.

Products that meet needs

The product, as we've said before, is so much more than a gizmo in a box. It's very easy to get fixated on the product (especially, it seems, for engineers), but you have to radically change your perspective. We hope the first few chapters have achieved this but, just in case, here's the reminder.

Customers don't buy products or even services, they buy the benefits. As we've already mentioned, innovation is a great strength in a small company. But it's not everything. In fact, most 'new' products aren't new products at all; they are simply reformulated or repackaged. Occasionally, they are simply relabelled. What makes a product different very often is the *way* it is 'delivered' to the customer. The core need being met is often the same, but there are extra benefits. As we'll see in Chapter 7, often that something extra is service, but it can just as easily be the perception or understanding of a product or a brand, the price (which is complex, as we see below) or how the product or service is accessed.

Large companies often spend a great deal of money researching and testing products. It's certainly true to say that short-cutting testing is a false economy. In many industries it's just foolish not to get approval from safety bodies or professional associations. Apart from the legal necessities, it's very often advisable to get independent professionals to assess and, if possible, endorse your product or service.

A company we dealt with specialised in very high-quality stainless steel fabrication. Sometimes it was metres of specially designed handrails for the entrance hall to a conference centre; the next job would be a one-off canopy for a new office building. They would be given a drawing and they made and fitted items to the specification provided.

How about . . . ?

. . . setting up a 'user group'. These can meet regularly to share experiences of the product. The group can be as formal or informal as you like, but you must keep control. Select participants carefully (see Chapter 3) as you want them to be able to speak openly in an atmosphere of co-operation.

Think about how they could be rewarded. Initially this may be simply by inviting them to a pleasant venue and offering food and refreshments. You can also offer them valuable information on how to use certain products or on relevant legislation.

Later, regular participants may be the first to be offered new products or services. In the software industry this is often referred to as 'beta testing' – before the product is finalised and made generally available.

If your customers are spread across a wide area, you might instead enable them to meet online, in which case you can have continuous feedback on your product or service.

Their problem was that they frequently presented to building contractors who bought primarily on price (design wasn't the most important element), and they could always be undercut. Rather than discounting, we advised them to build relationships with architects so that they could be specified as preferred suppliers for very high status (and high value) work.

Working closely with customers in the design of your product isn't confined to a 'research phase'. It can happen all the time: several companies set up customer panels to help them continuously improve. Even if no dramatic new ideas come out of these consultations, they involve customers and you are able to count them as loyal since they give not only their business, but also their time and intellect to you.

Even more integrated than this are the customers who are more than customers. When they join in designing and customising the product or service they buy, when you work in *their* offices and when a number of different suppliers also collaborate to fulfil your promise to them, customers are often more like partners. Again, as we shall see later, this is an enviable position to be in. From a strategic viewpoint, it also binds customers and suppliers together for the long term, effectively cutting out the competition.

The entire focus of what you produce and sell should be the customers' needs and wants. We know of a printing company that made it a point of honour always to say 'yes' to every job, no matter how outlandish or time-consuming. Sometimes it lost money on jobs it had never done before, like printing t-shirts or sourcing bolts of material for an exhibition stand. But the staff still said yes, and they learned. Far more important than the profit on each job was the profit inherent in the customer relationship. As the owner said, 'As long as they're your customer, you'll always have another job to make money on'.

The price is . . .

For many small companies, price is at once the simplest and yet often the most frustrating aspect of their business. It seems that if only the price was a little higher, they wouldn't have to work so hard to sell more. But just when it looks as though they're going to sell a lot, they get beaten down on the price.

Make no mistake, pricing is a strategic decision and it's far more than simply putting a price tag on the product. Because it is strategic, you have to spend considerable time on it before you approach customers.

Look at value, not cost

This is, perhaps, the simplest and best advice. If you have researched your customers and their needs, you'll begin to have some kind of grasp on the value they place on the product or service you offer. Following our advice from the earlier chapters, you will also have a good idea of why your offering is different (and better) than the competition. It is important not to underestimate this. Being better and cheaper is no strategy. Many customers use price as a shortcut to getting a fix on quality; in many cases, customers make a purchase decision based on *comparative* price so that, for example, they avoid the cheapest insurance policy but opt for the second most expensive as offering the best value – and that's usually without even reading the policy! Of course the 'best' customers (the ones we want) may simply go straight for the most expensive they can afford.

If you start off with the lowest price you can afford, it's almost impossible then to increase the price for the same customers without their starting to look elsewhere. It's also likely that, as a small company, you don't have the economies of scale that larger companies benefit from. If they decide to compete directly with you, they can undercut even your 'best' price. It's tough, but try to ensure that your early sales are at a reasonable price for *you* as well as for your customers. If you intend to offer a low price in order to penetrate the market quickly, then please make sure the actual discounted price is factored into your forecast income. In fact, whatever price you find you *can* get should be used to recalculate all the figures in your business plan.

Fix your price on the basis of what customers will pay, and what they ought to pay, if your product exactly meets their needs. It is hardly ever in your interests to calculate all your costs and then add a margin.

Break even means never having to hold a sale

The next thing to understand is the concept of break even. Once you have this firmly fixed in your mind, to the extent that you know your position at any given moment, you can begin to use pricing flexibly and to the advantage of your customers and your relationship with them.

To take a simple example (as it was taught to us many years ago), the greengrocer on her market stall can sell apples in the morning at £1 a kilo as the first customers arrive. Having bought them in the wholesale market, this equates to a profit of 50p per kilo. As the day wears on, the display becomes depleted, other stock is put out (and rearranged to best advantage) but, inevitably, the flow of customers slows. Towards the end of the day, with just a couple of boxes of apples left, our greengrocer drops the price to 40p.

Now we know there are many canny business people reading this who know why that price is right and could probably put together a good argument for not lowering the price or, indeed, throwing the last of the apples away. For those of you not so aware (and there is no shame in that – we regularly meet reasonably successful business people who aren't), the key is in knowing the break-even point:

- **Twenty cases of apples containing 10 kilos amounts to 200 kilos. At 50p per kilo, these cost £100 at the wholesalers.**
- **After selling 100 kilos at £1, the greengrocer has reached break even – anything sold *at any price* now makes profit.**
- **After a few hours, having sold 160 kilos, the greengrocer has made £60 profit.**
- **The remaining 40 kilos can still be sold *at any price* and still generate more profit.**

The issue here is that the price is fundamental to the strategy of the business. So what do you want to achieve?

If you want to maximise profit, then you *have* to sell *all* the apples at the best possible price at the time. In reality that means lowering the price until all the apples go. The customers in the morning are not the same as those in the afternoon and the market is not the same. If you want to maintain your reputation for high-quality apples (apart from the fact you have sorted through them and already thrown some away – a loss), you may go through the whole day at the same price and run the risk of not selling some.

If your aim is to be a good citizen, then you may already have an arrangement with a couple of local schools to donate small amounts of surplus to them each week.

Knowing the break-even point opens up possibilities.

How about...?

... working out some break-even figures for your business. The calculation is simple and will be used over and over again as your costs and prices change.

Simply calculate your fixed costs – those that you must pay every day, week or month, such as mortgage or rent, staff costs, utility bills and so on.

Choose a time-basis for your calculation that you feel comfortable with. If you can only look a week ahead, then deal with a week at a time.

In order to establish the profitability of the week as you go along, take the value of each job and subtract the direct or variable costs that are associated only with that job. You may have to estimate this if, for example, you use only a portion of materials bought for the job.

The resulting figure is a contribution to your overheads.

> Once you have enough jobs in the week to cover your overheads, then you can begin to make profit.
>
> Your only concern then is that each job is priced to cover its direct costs.
>
> Can you then use this 'flexible pricing' to reward regular customers, get more work from them or to encourage new customers?

Yes, but we have no bananas

Now, before you go arguing that you're not into fruit and veg, let us remind you that exactly the same logic applies to airline seats, solicitors and plumbers. In fact, the same logic can be applied to all kinds of business. Why?

Well firstly, for greengrocers and for any kind of service, the product is totally perishable. If it's not sold today, it can't be sold at all. The plumber who has eight hours a day to 'sell' may book out four hours on one job and then spend an hour travelling, leaving three hours unsold. Those hours may represent his profit, and they can't be resold tomorrow.

On the other hand, if you start to add up the plumber's overheads and costs on a monthly basis and can see that these are covered by week three, you can have a week of profit making! In that week you can do an awful lot of good to your business. Imagine facing a new customer during that 'profit-making' week. 'Well,' you might say, 'if you can give me the order now, I can do it at £X.' X may be at cost or it may even be lower than that since your overheads may include a budget for gaining a new customer (see Chapter 6).

Money off?

Having brought up the subject of discounting, we need to make our views plain. Discounting must always be strategic. Price is such a powerful signal to customers that to play with it is risky. If you have sales people who feel they have to give discounts just to get the business, then perhaps they (or you) don't understand the business you are in.

If your price is higher than your competitors, there has to be a good reason for it. It may be that other suppliers are cheaper than you because they're more profitable and want to undercut you. It may be that they are losing money and don't realise themselves how important pricing is. Many companies have arrived in a marketplace in a blaze of publicity and discounted pricing, only to disappear again as rapidly. In order to justify your price, you very often have to resort to honesty. Sometimes this is tough, but if you have the kind of relationship we referred to above where you work closely with your customers, there is no reason why you shouldn't tell them how much profit you need to make. In some cases, relationships are so good that customers and suppliers run so-called 'open' accounting systems. In these, prices are agreed, costs are known and profit is seen as a natural and fair result of the business relationship.

In other businesses, we know, it can be a struggle to maintain prices and profit. In this situation, you need to be very close to your customers (as we suggest in Chapter 5) and to develop your product with their needs and wants in mind. Often, taking a longer-term view of a relationship and accepting that it goes through phases means that you can budget accordingly. The initial investment phase while you build and cement the relationship will not be profitable, but then as you become a more important and relied-upon supplier, profit can be 'engineered' into each successive job. Sometimes it's necessary to take a loss on one product or service in order to secure a more profitable subsequent job.

But I'm different

If your business doesn't seem to figure in what we've just said about pricing, it may be that you find it difficult to see how you can be flexible in this area. Very often in retailing, prices are comparatively stable – and closely monitored by your competitors. Sometimes it's possible to use price as the basis for promotion. Almost every supermarket and off-licence has some form of promotional pricing that enables them to advertise headline prices on 'reference' items. Such items vary with different product sectors and at different times, hence the off-licence will aim to offer an apparently good deal on beer in the run up to a World Cup match.

Bearing in mind what we've said about pricing on the basis of value, you might also want to consider whether you should really offer discounts of any sort to *all* customers. Far better to use the same expenditure (and you can look at such discounts as marketing costs to you) in order to reward certain high-value customers (such as those you identified in Chapters 2 and 3). You can do this with membership schemes and preferred customer cards, which may also have the effect of encouraging loyalty.

If you're concerned that the issues we've dealt with ignore organisations that don't aim to make a profit, then maybe you really don't understand pricing. Remember pricing is as much about communicating value as it is about income and profit. If you have to promote a theatre performance or set the price for a charity sponsorship deal, then you still need to influence the perception of its value. We can hardly launch into a full description of both arts and charity marketing here, but the principles are largely the same. We would argue, of course, that you need to make a surplus on most, if not all, activities to raise money for a cause or at the very least to secure your organisation's future when funding may not be so readily available.

A problem shared

A company we visited developed a new product simply to sell its existing product range.

Many car servicing workshops are untidy, dirty places. The company supplied them with small parts and consumables but found that they were selling primarily on price and speed of delivery.

Rather than accept the situation, they developed a bespoke racking system for their products that made it easier for their customers to monitor and reorder stock.

To sell it into the garages they commissioned research that showed the cost savings of having products in stock and easily accessible. This was a compelling reason for garages to consider investing in the new system.

The 'deal closer' was that the company offered the racking *free*, in return for ongoing business that the garage was planning anyway.

> The garages couldn't lose and the auto supplies company gained more loyal customers, along with a reason to visit them regularly to see how the racking performed.

In these cases, price discounting to targeted customers or groups of customers can then fulfil the mission of widening access to the arts or encouraging commitment from less well-off donors. In this case, the concept of a break-even still applies, except that the figure is based on a required surplus – subsequent sales can then be used as a particularly powerful promotional tool.

I'm sorry, we're full

It never ceases to amaze us that the importance of the break-even calculation is missed by even the most professional of organisations. Small businesses are able to make decisions quickly enough (we hope) to avoid this.

If your restaurant receives an enquiry for a table for 15 on one of your busiest nights, what do you do? In some cases, there's nothing you can do: if you're fully booked, you're fully booked. But you should be able at least to offer another date (when the restaurant is less busy). In fact, it's likely you have two or three, maybe more, evenings when your takings don't even cover the staff costs. You might eventually cover these costs on Friday and Saturday, but here is a perfect case for flexible pricing. You can offer incentives for booking earlier in the week and it needn't be as obvious as 'book for two, pay only for one meal'.

By talking to those people who do come earlier in the week, you can find out why and you can encourage them to come again, and bring friends. Even a coffee or dessert 'on the house' because you spend time chatting with them (because you're not busy) might have the desired effect. One restaurant owner made a point of telling customers on Monday that it was his favourite night ('the customers are so much nicer') and then did the same on Tuesday and Wednesday.

A more overt way would be to have a distinct menu early in the week that is cheaper but simpler, perhaps a 'tasting' menu or a 'seasonal' menu where there is a range of dishes but customers try every one. In effect, you treat the early part of the week as a different market, indeed a different business.

Forget about price

Finally, our last piece of advice on pricing ties in with our first; always focus on the value of what you offer. However the other side of the coin is that the *cost to your customer* isn't always monetary.

If you think back to the concept of the value chain, much of what your customers have to do in order to buy your product may seem to be free – at least there doesn't seem to be a cost that *you* need to take into account. Your customers may have a different view. If the product isn't quite what they wanted, there's a cost to them (technically, they forego some of the 'utility' they anticipated), but if yours is available and the preferred alternative is not then this reduces the perceived cost (of waiting or searching further a field). Your customers may have to drive a long way to find you, or they may find it time consuming to work out where your showroom is. These are costs – some do have monetary value as well but most are 'time-costs'.

Price connects directly with customers' perception of risk too. It is extremely powerful to offer the product with a 'money-back guarantee' or 'free on approval' option and, as long as the (surprisingly low) costs of this kind of offer are factored in, this can deal with many issues around price.

The more you can address the customer's concerns about cost (time and money) with excellent service, indeed even reinventing your service, the better. You'll be able to justify charging a higher price to boot.

Convenience

Much of what we have just said about price interlinks with the idea of customer convenience. Just making it easier for customers to say 'yes' is a great inducement to purchase.

Customers constantly weigh up the pros and cons of a purchase; all the more so in the top half of the Holden-Wilde matrix, where they perceive the cost to be significant. If you can take away barriers and remove areas of uncertainty, you can boost sales and strengthen your pricing. Perhaps the best example for such items is offering finance or stage payments. Customers can then gain the immediate benefit of your product or service at a minimal immediate cost. If you do offer these deals (even if they are 'interest free'), you must check out the relevant legislation. There are specialist finance companies who can offer you branded finance products (and which have the necessary regulatory approvals to do so). The Office of Fair Trading gives some useful guidance[4].

How convenient can you make it?

It used to be that marketers talked about distribution, but like most things, it got more complicated. Getting a product from manufacturer to customer is not simply a case of transport or opening a store. The logistics needed to transport even relatively simple products like food are fraught with rules and regulations that often confound small businesses. It is often necessary to find a partner business that already has an established distribution network for a similar, but complementary rather than competitive, product. The advantages will be huge. Apart from learning about their business as you go, you may well be giving *them* a product to offer to *their* clients.

If your business needs to invest heavily in distribution, then a visit to the Institute of Logistics and Transport[5] may be in order.

Retailing and distribution is a whole subject for another book, but if you are guided by the essential principles earlier on, you may find that you have already made key decisions. For a physical product, the aim is simply for it to be where customers need it. For most small businesses, this means using existing distribution networks, including wholesalers and retailers, as we have already mentioned.

It's worth considering these networks too as your customers. What does your product offer to these important members of your value chain that they cannot get elsewhere? Getting to grips with this means that you have to understand their business in the same way that you try to understand your own (end user) customers. You should probably develop a marketing plan just for these.

A large retailer will see no value in giving over shelf space to another brand of pet food unless there is already demonstrable demand. In reality, therefore, if your product is in a market already well served by mainstream products, you will have to find an alternative distribution 'channel' – at least until you build up your track record and can approach the retailer again. The Dog Deli mentioned earlier is an example of this first stage of a developing distribution plan.

If you do get distribution of any kind, it's as well to remember that you are dealing with other businesses each with their own plans and needs. They will therefore expect to make a profit on your product. Frequently small businesses approach larger chain stores or distributors with unrealistic expectations. If you have a retail price in mind for your product, it's likely you will receive no more than 50% and possibly nearer 25% of that in order to give them acceptable margins. This clearly has an impact on your profitability and your marketing plan. But remember 25% of a lot is better than 100% of nothing.

Beware geeks bearing gifs[6]

Not everything can be a dot-com. Amid the understandable excitement regarding the Internet and the possibilities for business, it's easy to forget some of the fundamentals. When an entrepreneur says 'Hey, I've got a great idea', it's usually about making something available online. 'Why don't we . . .

- **sell cars online**
- **sell records online**
- **offer divorces online**
- **open a coffee shop online?'**

Of course, these all pose problems for different reasons.

- **Cars are already sold online, but you still have to deliver them and, understandably, some people are reluctant to take the condition of a car on trust without (as they say) kicking the tyres.**
- **Records are sold online – djfriendly is a particularly entertaining site[7] – but the music industry is still grappling with the fact that music doesn't have to be physically delivered as Spotify has shown. Any product that can be digitised is now being revolutionised by**

communications technology – photography, music and, most of all, information.

- You can get some services online – legal and financial services are becoming more accessible – but it's a matter of degree. Documents still have to be signed and witnessed and, for many people, there is still a need to sit across a desk face to face. However, things are changing and relatively complex legal issues such as house buying and mortgages are taking place online; the only things that need to be physically are documents.

Of course there are some things that can't be delivered online, where the experience cannot be as multi-sensory as the real world equivalent. The day fresh coffee is digitised is the day to sell your shares in the transport industry. Operating your business online can create distance where none need exist . . . and it makes it impossible for your customer to touch or smell the product.

The main point to make about all distribution is that it is necessary only in as much as it adds value for your customers. Sometimes that means it is essential in order to put the product in your customers' hands, but asking those 'what if' questions of this area, you frequently come up with interesting answers. In businesses where it is customary to deal at a distance, then being close to customers may be an advantage. Where customers are expected to get close to a supplier, then the opportunity to deal at a distance (perhaps online) may be attractive to some customers.[8]

Here again, your strategy has to be built on some information. Are there enough such customers? Is that what they really want and are they prepared to pay for it?

Don't shout; you'll do yourself an injury!

The most over-rated business is advertising. It's such a visible part of our entertainment industry (yes, that is what we wrote) that we tend to idolise it as well as, on occasions, vilify it.

Advertising, like any industry, is driven by companies (agencies and media owners) trying to gain business and make profit. Small companies tend not to have much business or profit to give them. It's worth remembering that advertising agencies grew up around the newspaper industry and their main job was to sell space; in other words they were generating business for the media.

It's changed quite a lot since then, but essentially for the small business owner, mass media needs you more than you need it. Rather than try and make a big noise in national newspapers, television or radio, we recommend you try and talk to customers, face-to-face if possible. If you can also let them touch your product and try it and taste it, then immediately you are more real than the half-page two-colour ad on page 4 of the local paper. It's not that we want to discourage you from promoting your business (you'll find plenty on this in the following chapters), we just want to inoculate you against the idea that promotion = advertising.

As we said early on, you can't compete with the biggest businesses directly. If the supermarkets and banks choose to fight it out in the national media, you need to choose your battle-ground more carefully. In any case, while advertising undoubtedly works, it does so by repetition and by entertaining. In the long term, it can make companies, products and brands famous and therefore more familiar to customers (familiar in the way that David and Victoria Beckham are 'familiar' to consumers; but they're not customers' best friends).

Your challenge takes place in the space between you and your customers. Make this distance small, and it's difficult for anyone to get between you, even (perhaps especially) Tesco. Make sure that your customers talk to you (and you listen) as much as you talk to them and they may consider you as more important than just a supplier.

As we shall see in the next two chapters, dealing directly with your own customers is the logical strategy for marketing on a shoestring. If we wanted to be academic about this, we'd call it direct and relationship marketing.

Remember . . . everything!

The issues around customer needs and wants, the costs that they face, their convenience and their communications needs are important and, as we've shown, interdependent. It is impossible to consider one without also considering its effect on the others. It's also impossible to think about these elements of your marketing plan without also being absolutely clear which customers you are addressing.

As we have suggested, your strategy may involve addressing two or more kinds of customer. If these customers require different things (even if it is only a different way of communicating) then they *are* different and should have a distinct plan.

For example,

For our Gold Card customers we will develop three exclusive exercise and therapy classes to be run on Tuesday nights (7pm, 7.30pm and 8pm). These will be 'taster' sessions including toning, pilates, boxercise, kinesiology, meditation and reiki. These will be offered at £1 (25% of the standard class price) for 30 minutes. Customers will be invited to pay £52 at the time of membership renewal. Ad hoc attendance will be charged at £4.

Standard members will be offered Gold membership upgrades after 6 months with the incentive to run on a further 12 months.

To promote new memberships . . .

A 'B2B' marketer might set out his or her tactical plans like this:

Our A list customers will be personally invited to our Summer Exhibition where they will be presented the new developments in our 'wireflow' process. Each will have a member of staff allocated to them and a personal demonstration of the process and will receive a copy of the cost-saving calculation based on their current usage.

We will make appointments to visit their premises to verify their work throughput and refine our calculations. At this stage we will show how the new machine will release floor space.

The detailed decisions you make about how you treat customers are, of course, important. But they are not, in themselves, strategy; nor are they once-and-for-all decisions.

As you put your plan into action, things will change. You will learn and you may then decide to change something about the product; you may have to introduce flexible pricing or offer discounts to certain customers. You may find that your distribution method is not generating enough business and you need to add other channels. You may find that your letter to your customers doesn't get the response you'd hoped for.

All these things will happen and you will respond.

Among all this, your strategy, as outlined early on in this chapter, will remain. Remember it's long-term and important. Your strategy plugs straight into the aims and ambitions for your business.

Of course it is possible, after many a bump and scrape, for you to realise that your strategy is flawed. In this case it can *only* be because something you put into it was wrong, perhaps based on inadequate research. We will deal with this in Chapter 7, but for the moment we hope you are developing your strategy on the basis of the best information you can get – currently.

What next?

Go back over your strategy and you will identify ideas and suggestions for the next stage; the action plan to make it happen. You may have too many ideas at this stage (remember the 'ideas box'?), or you may find you have an objective or strategy that seems to be unrealistic. If this is the case, you need to break down the strategy into the components you used to build it – what was it you hoped to achieve? What was the insight (perhaps from your research) that led you to this point? If in doubt, take the advice in Chapter 3 and above to talk with customers and get them involved in designing your product and service.

You will, no doubt, go around the process of developing a strategy several times until you are happy with it. As you go on to the next chapters, your plan will still be somewhat tentative, but you should be getting ever more confident about how to implement it and the objectives you have set.

Notes/References

1. That's not an excuse to avoid writing anything down, it's just that a few companies actually run on pictures – images and 'vibes' that the owners share.

If you're in this position don't forget that as you grow, you'll be compelled to collaborate with people who don't have your visual imagination so a written plan will help. It's not a bad thing to wonder what would happen to the company if you were to get hit by the proverbial bus tomorrow.

2. 90 posts   5 applicants   30-minute interview = 225 hours = 5   40-hour weeks! And that's just the interviewing . . .

3. The 4Ps are, as you may know, Product, Price, Place and Promotion. The formula is old and . . . well, formulaic. Nevertheless some kind of mnemonic is useful and the one we prefer is the 4Cs – Customer needs and wants, Cost to the consumer, Convenience and Communication. The originators were Don Shultz, Stanley Tannenbaum and Robert Lauterborn in *The New Marketing Paradigm, Integrated Marketing Communications* (1994), NTC Business Books/McGraw Hill.

4. *www.oft.gov.uk*

5. *www.ciltuk.org.uk*

6. We're sure this isn't original. If anyone can tell us where it comes from, we'll credit it. If not, we'll accept the glory.

7. *www.djfriendly.co.uk*

8. You might like to check out *Virtually Free Marketing* (by Phil Holden and published by, Bloomsbury Publishing Plc) which discusses online options in much more detail.

5
KEEPING CUSTOMERS

In this chapter, we'll look at how to keep existing customers and ways of growing your business. We will focus on searching for the right information and also consider ways of understanding customer requirements.

We suggest ways of improving communication with customers and the importance of constantly trying to improve customer service. We also show how you can make decisions about expenditure on existing customers by understanding customer lifetime value (LTV).

Customers are just people

As we said at the outset, marketing is essentially about building the whole of your business around customers, and that means getting in as close and as personal as they will let you. It's been said that you gain customers with product and you retain them with service. Up to a point that's true. We'll see in the next chapter how important it is to go about recruiting the right sort of customers, but why think about keeping customers before you've gained them? It's because you need to target customers based on what they need; it's not about what you happen to have available to sell.

Just for a moment, think about the future of your business. You've worked hard to win over new customers; what could affect their relationship with you in the future? What would you have to do to allow somebody to take away those customers … perhaps just as you did? The answer is 'not very much'; neglecting your customers or taking them for granted.

As you'll see, we think the best information about potential new customers very often comes from existing customers so, for example, if you only have one customer, think about how you found her, why she uses you (and not your competitors) and how much she is worth to your business – quite a lot … in fact 100% of your business!

You don't need a huge marketing plan to try and get one more customer like her – and grow your business another 100%. You are in this position if your work over the previous chapters has shown that you have one or two customers accounting for most, if not all, of your income or profit. You need to hold on to them, then maybe find one more exactly like them.

For many companies there is the 80:20 rule. One company we met were convinced they needed new customers because their biggest one (Marks & Spencer) accounted for 70% of their turnover. They were right, but they *also* needed to avoid the loss of this one customer that could sink the business.

Not surprisingly, most companies we meet with think they need new customers. Actually what they often need is more income and more profit. And the easiest new business to win is from customers who already know and like you. The reason companies need new customers is usually because they are convinced that they can't possibly sell any more to their existing customers. The biggest culprits are usually those sales people who try to sell exclusively via the phone. When asked to push for more business, they phone down the list of customers they haven't contacted for a while and ask them if they're 'looking for anything'. It's easy for the customer to say no, and there you have it: conclusive evidence that we can't do any more business with this client!

Think about it for a moment. The customers you know most about are those you work with day after day. Your best customers are those who come back to you time after time. So the first thing to discover is why these 'best' customers buy what you sell. We want you to think carefully about this before you start phoning and finding out why. Perhaps you have never actually discussed your working relationship with your clients. Why should you? You contact them or they contact you, an order is placed and delivered and they pay on time and that is it. Well, see if they can find time to meet you and have a more open and frank discussion.

Knowing the truth from your customers

Some of the best marketing intelligence comes from *within* your company. You also need to think carefully about how you gather and evaluate this information (see Chapter 3) but the information you, or others, hold in their files (or in their memories) relating to customers is *essential* and must never be thrown away. You could argue that the knowledge you hold is an asset with a real financial value. Many large companies do in fact try and value and manage this with whole departments devoted to 'knowledge management'. Small companies don't. How many times does a reasonably successful entrepreneur acknowledge the importance of personal knowledge as they tap their head and tell you that 'it's all up here' – which can be frustrating for anyone else, particularly if you're new to the company or trying to pick up the reins of a family firm.

The solution is to share knowledge as openly and freely as is possible. Some small companies are every good at this. They talk about customers, about orders as they are fulfilled, problems and complaints as well as good ideas. Again, this is a process that many larger companies would regard with envy – it's almost impossible to share all the experience of all the 'customer-facing' staff across a huge multinational. If you are in that position, then you're lucky. If not, then you need to get there.

To change the way you work isn't easy. If your sales people are shut away while they're making calls, try to get round that. The people who manage your key accounts are holding vital parts of your business in their hands and there's some research to suggest that internal barriers between these people and the rest can lose you business[1].

What kind of information?

Remember this table from Chapter 2?

Customers			
	% turnover	% profit	% of their requirements
Daly's	12	15	50
BAe	30	15	5
Askew Engineering	17	32	70
Monitor Retail Systems	4	1	100
Skane Engineering	15	21	10
Rutherford & Co	2	6	30
Lucas	20	10	1

AbraCAD Engineering

We only added the most basic of information from our own records – the importance of the customer to our turnover and the profit margin on the work we do for them.

Previously, we might have looked at BAe and Lucas as the biggest customers; they account for half the value of our invoices. In a typical small company, these would be key accounts.

Then we might have considered Daly's, Askew and Skane as the 'second tier' customers and Monitor and Rutherford as the bottom tier. Alternatively, you might look at Askew and Skane as the best simply because their jobs generate a lot of profit.

But then, in the final column, we've estimated what percentage of *their* total needs we are currently meeting and this changes everything.

This last piece of information may not be very accurate. After all, you may realistically not be able to do all the work that a big client like BAe or Lucas needs. But, realistically, what could you do for them? Looking just at the products or services you are already delivering, are these all that this customer buys? You can often get some insight into this simply by talking to customers and some of the research sources in Chapter 3 might help.

Now, you can begin to prioritise in a slightly different way. By looking at the potential each customer has for growth and then just multiplying the figures across the table gives you an indication of their comparative value.

We use the 'potential figure' (the one in brackets in the table overleaf) to recognise the importance of growing our customers. Monitor is clearly less important in this regard than Daly's or Skane.

Please don't go thinking these are magic numbers: they just enable a *comparison* of the potential value of a customer.

AbraCAD Engineering

Customer	% turnover	% profit	% of their requirements (% potential)	Product of three factors =
Daly's	12	15	50 (50)	9000
BAe	30	15	5 (95)	42750
Askew Engineering	17	32	70 (30)	16320
Monitor Retail Systems	4	1	100 (0)	4
Skane Engineering	15	21	10 (90)	28350
Rutherford & Co	2	6	30 (70)	840
Lucas	20	10	1 (99)	19800

You can also make all these easier to compare by turning the last figure into an 'index' figure. Take the largest figure (in this case BAe), divide by 100 (resulting in 1% of the highest figure) and divide each of the other figures by the result. You get an indication of this as follows.

AbraCAD: Ranking of customers

	Index
BAe	100
Skane Engineering	66
Lucas	46
Askew Engineering	38
Daly's	21
Rutherford & Co	2
Monitor Retail Systems	0

The conclusion here has to be that we really need to know what Skane want. BAe and Lucas are major names that all our competitors probably target, but Skane is 'our' customer ... and we want to befriend them.

We're not, for a moment, suggesting you throw away the basic figures you used to generate this. In the spirit of sharing all information that could help you make decisions, you should show all your colleagues (and anyone else whose opinion you trust – and whom you can trust with this dynamite information) and get them to work out their own versions. Do they tell a different story?

Again remember the principle. There isn't one way of doing this. How you go about this is as important as the final answer. If your competitors are chasing Lucas but ignoring Skane, you've got some kind of advantage.

How about . . .?

Checking what data you already have. If you deal with private individuals as customers, check that you have written permission to use it as you wish. If not, get it.

This may be an opportunity to contact customers again, so don't pass on it. You want to know from them how they'd like to be contacted.

One charity that did this got more donations as a result of only contacting donors once a year, when they requested it rather than sending all their contacts every appeal.

We're all individuals

In the case of a retailer with many customers you might try and estimate the figures above for groups of similar customers. In most marketing textbooks these are called 'segments' but we prefer the term 'clusters'. The difference is simply that segmentation is very often imposed on a whole market while clusters should arise from the characteristics of customers as you discover them. Principally, you discover these through research; more or less formal.

It's reasonable to ask one in every hundred customers to fill in a questionnaire, but as we've intimated before, you have to be careful how you select respondents and what questions you ask. You also have to be cautious about how you use the information[2].

Once you start collecting and using customer data you should, in principle, be seeking permission to use this data. We say 'in principle' because some larger (and some smaller, less honest) companies are fairly lax about getting unequivocal permission from customers. Some use data supplied by a third party and don't enquire too closely about its origins.

We believe that small companies almost always have an advantage over larger companies in this area. Collecting data as an exercise on its own is difficult, but collecting it in the course of your everyday interaction with customers is much easier. Again it's vital that everyone knows the importance of both collecting and, just as crucial, recording this information. Simply listening to what your customers say is vital to the future of a small business.

Carrying out research on existing customers

Building on the research techniques we introduced in Chapter 3, you now need to start researching your existing customers. They might be pleased to speak to researchers or they may be guarded and defensive. Using an independent researcher might encourage them to talk more openly.

If you have just a few customers, then a semi-structured interview that allows you to explore key areas of service will suffice, but if you are using a sample then you will need to build in some mechanisms for comparing reactions such as Likert scales, where you ask them to rate items on a scale of 1–5. Our own preference is to try and do an in-depth interview with customers, if time permits, and then decide how to proceed. If you do have competitors, then build in similar questions about them. Have you ever been compared on a scale of 1–5 with your closest competitor? If they rank you as 3 and them as 4, then there is reparation work to be done (and incidentally it doesn't mean you have to be 30% better – you need to identify the differences and address them).

If you analyse the results and record them, then they might be used for staff training or to help inform future decisions about customers. If your scores fall below a certain level, then it is time to draw up an action plan and get to the root of the problems.

Constant communication with customers

For some companies, the only communication they look forward to from customers is the cheque in response to an invoice. We've even visited companies where the sales people didn't like to go and see customers and so stayed at their desks all week making plans! It is a particular problem where the market is split into territories. Do I really want to make that journey to a customer who is the furthest away, when quite frankly we get as much as we possibly can from them just by telephoning them?

One of the principles of good customer relations is that communication has to work both ways. In fact it's part of the definition of direct and relationship marketing.

A company that takes relationships with its customers seriously has to listen (and respond) to customers as well as talking to them. In our experience in a marketing communications agency, clients frequently expected an advert or brochure to sell without any thought for what the customers actually wanted. As you know from the very first chapter of this book – that's not what marketing is about.

So, in order to really know your customers you have to monitor every communication with each customer. If you can, you should capture and track every contact with every customer and potential customer. This is often a logistical nightmare for even very small businesses let alone those with thousands of customers.

If you have just a handful of customers or even a few hundred, it's worth persevering with a plan to capture as much information as you can. It is surprising how much information you can pick up from trade magazines and from news websites. It makes sense to do regular searches on your customers. If you are able to talk to them about future plans that you found on their website, then it at least shows that you are taking an interest in them.

Much of the key data you collect can be captured on very simple spreadsheets or, for the more computer literate, simple database programs such as Microsoft Access. Microsoft even has a part of their website devoted to small businesses that may help[3].

To start with however, you can do some quick analysis with pen and paper. Let's have a look at a very simple chart with data from five companies.

	Service	Delivery	Customer Service	Technical Support	Comments
Company A	4	5	4	3	Can't always get through to telephone support number
Company B	4	3	3	3	By far one of our best suppliers
Company C	5	4	3	1	Technical support can be quite obstructive and difficult to deal with
Company D	4	4	4	4	
Company E	5	4	3	2	We have unresolved issues with technical support, but overall service is very good

In this case companies A, B and C could be our customers while D and E are served by one of our competitors. For this we're using the Likert scale again where, in this case, 5 means 'totally satisfied' and 1 is 'completely dissatisfied'.

We have to be careful not to read too much into these findings at this stage but still deal with the pressing issues. What is the problem between technical support and company C? Perhaps there is a problem with technical support that we don't know about? Have we reviewed our customer service training for all of our support staff? We must investigate the problem immediately. Is technical support an issue for most companies, and is it therefore an opportunity for us to take the lead in this area? One small business used to send out 'job sheets' detailing the work done, which in effect were questionnaires, in order to encourage regular feedback.

Of course some of this analysis is easier, or at least quicker if you need to carry it out repeatedly, on a computer system.

A word of warning. No computer system is going to make marketing decisions for you, so you have to have in mind a plan of the kind of information you need before you plunge into buying software. If you've started with pen and paper as we've suggested, then you may have a good idea of the kind of system you need. Once you have an idea of what the system has to do for you, you can then try and give this benefit a value.

This is important since any investment in computer software should be an investment in your company and not Bill Gates's. Keep asking yourself, is it worth it? Some of the issues below under 'data driven marketing' will help you.

If you're determined to buy something complex, then like all purchases, you have to do your homework[4]. Local business computer suppliers *may* be able to give you advice, but don't assume they understand your business. And don't even assume that they understand the software you're interested in; they often don't have time to really use the software they sell.

Remember that software isn't a one-off purchase. Once you have it you will have to learn to use it (a time-cost at least), use it (an overhead probably since it will be an additional admin task) and you have to upgrade fairly often. If your software lasts three years without revision, you've done well.

A good source of information is from networks such as business clubs, Business Link organisations and Chambers of Commerce. Here again, be careful. Rather than simply look at what advice they offer, you should try and use them, or your own contacts, to get in touch with similar companies to your own who have already successfully implemented a similar software solution. What *measurable* benefits it has brought about (has their £3,000 system brought in more than £3,000 of profit?). It's also a good idea to speak to people who use the system without the boss looking over their shoulder. Their honest opinion may be quite revealing.

Data-driven marketing

There's no doubt that direct marketing has enjoyed phenomenal growth over the last ten years. You have probably noticed that more and more of the companies you deal with (as a private customer) communicate by mail, by phone and of course by e-mail. Your bank, insurance company, even your local council, probably conducts much of its business electronically.

The key issue is that the interactions between the company and its customers can be managed online and consist of pretty simple data. If you're towards the right-hand side of our matrix then you might welcome the ability to deal with many customers efficiently.

Concrete takes flight

SMC Mini-Mix decided to be different. They deliver ready-mixed concrete to over 600 regular accounts (and an increasing number of domestic customers) in the West Midlands. The company offers a 'helpful driver and wheelbarrow at no extra cost'. This simple difference overcomes the problems associated with taking delivery of concrete and sets the company apart from its competitors.

But diaries and card indices bulged with addresses and telephone numbers, so staff had to constantly call the boss for details of customers and there was much duplication of effort in maintaining the manual systems. Partner Richard Timmis admitted, 'I'm not particularly IT literate but I knew that the lack of a good customer management system was causing an obstacle to our growth. All our credit customers are now on the Flightdeck system and all staff have instant access to the information. This has proved to be motivational and it's a great sales management tool. We can view on screen which customers have placed orders and when they are scheduled to go out. We even have virtual sales meetings by telephone with our field representative. He has access to Flightdeck from his home office so that we can discuss his activity at the end of each week while we both look at the records on screen.'

Reproduced with kind permission of Software Sculptors www. flightdeckcrm.co.uk

The problems arise, as we shall see below, when the service encounter is actually made *more* difficult by the systems you have in place, whether these are technological or human. It doesn't have to be difficult. At Gatwick airport we used the pay-as-you go Internet service. We encountered some problems, pointed out that we had in fact lost £2 in the machine, and we were given a credit voucher immediately. Clearly they had a 'no quibble' policy and simply refunded the money and generated a certain amount of goodwill.

Try to put some value on your customer's time when you are servicing products. True, you made money when you sold it to them, you have provided a certain level of service, but now things are going wrong with the machine, which you have accepted might be the fault of your company, then resolve it without taking up too much of their time. Don't ask them to fill out extra forms, or make them wait three days, or insist that they bring their new machine in. Remember that a 'quibble free' approach to refunds and repairs is a good way of retaining customers.

Your planning options for customer data look something like this –

RELATIVELY	Few customers Infrequent purchase	Many customers More frequent purchase
Large transactions (from the point of view of the customer)	Essential to track individual customers But can be low-tech	Essential, but must be very cost-efficient Probably computer-based
Small transactions (from the point of view of the customer)	Important, but must be low cost possibly computer-based but 'off the shelf'	Less important and must be very cost-efficient

The small retailer in the bottom right can't have a computer system tracking customers, but it could recognise that there are certain clusters of customer that must be tracked. If your shop sells luggage, for example, is there a corporate market that you can serve positioned towards the top left of the grid? This is a separate market and may indeed be (or become) a separate business. You need to have a list of these corporate clients (and potential clients) and invest time in maintaining your links with them. You could phone them periodically to see if the contact you have is current ('Does Sam Smith still look after buying gifts for clients?' Remember their DMU?).

With more valuable customers the balance changes. Keeping such customers is vital – how many do you need to track and can it be done (reliably) manually?

Should you have a website?

We cannot think of a business that won't benefit by having a Web presence. Almost all the companies we now come into contact with have some kind of Web presence and the chances are it's one of the things you thought about at the same time as you considered letter headings and the name of your company.

If you haven't already got a website, or you find yourself in a company that doesn't take the Internet seriously, then you should make this a priority. The use of the Web is such a big issue we can't possibly do it justice here. We'd advise you to buy a copy of Phil's excellent book, *Virtually Free Marketing* (Bloomsbury Publishing Plc) which explains (virtually) all.

Again, think about your position (both actual and desired) on the Holden-Wilde matrix. If you're dealing with many customers making small purchases, every so often they'll want to find out your phone number or address. For many people this new means Web first, phone directory later. If you can automate aspects of your service, you may be helping customers. You can have a website on a shoestring – so do it!

As you look at your strategy to (also) address higher value customers a website becomes even more essential. But increasingly it's the case with even low-value products and services (in the bottom left corner) that need to be convenient. Why can't your local newsagent allow you to change your newspaper order online and pay by credit card or direct debit? Why shouldn't its whole stock be online so that a customer can see if they've run out of semi-skimmed milk or nappies at 10pm on a Sunday?

Of course the Web can do so much more and there is a case for saying that it can revolutionise small business marketing. Several thousand small companies now derive most of their income simply from their 'store' on the massive online auction site Ebay.

It's the system . . .

A certain phone company in the UK (OK, it's BT) regularly sends its customers a bill with the happy news that they are in credit along with the reassuring message (and we quote):

'Your account is in credit, which means your monthly payments are greater than your total charges for this statement. You don't need to take any further action, as your payments will continue to be collected as normal. If we need to change your payment amount we will advise you.'

So, of course, you should immediately phone them and ask for your payments to be reduced AND start looking for a cheaper deal. What they should be saying is:

'We notice you're paying too much for your phone. So we won't be collecting any payment from you for the next two months. We hope you enjoy spending this money on something more worthwhile and interesting than your phone bill.

If you'd rather pay it to us then just call us, free, on 0800 12345678, or fill in the slip below and pop it in the post.'

Incidentally, the last time this happened, BT owed one of us £132 and proposed to keep taking £39 a month – we negotiated it to £15 . . . and then changed suppliers.

Budgeting to keep your customers

Let us start by explaining why looking after customers is so important (which might seem quite obvious) and how you can go about measuring its importance in pounds and pence.

Lifetime value (LTV)

LTV is a really powerful concept to always consider when you carry out marketing activities.

It helps overcome the problem of budgeting marketing expenditure over the long term when you normally set budgets year by year. For example, you may know that your best customers have been with you for years but it's less easy to know how profitable they have been (on their own) over those years. How much should you spend on recruiting a customer this year who you know will buy products over ten years and maybe, just maybe, make his biggest purchase in six years time?

If that sounds unlikely, consider a security firm that specialised in commercial properties (we'll call them *Gotcha* Security Ltd). Contacting companies to sell them a security system was like pulling teeth. 'We've already got one' was the most frequent answer. Instead they marketed their maintenance, security checks and generally lower-value products like locks and keys.

The long term aim was to develop trusting relationships with some very big clients. Then, when these clients realised that they needed a new system, the security firm was in a perfect position to tender.

Incidentally, *Gotcha* didn't have the benefit of comparing themselves on the Holden-Wilde matrix! But if they had, they would have seen their strategy identifying higher-value, less frequent purchases.

The problem this firm actually had was that the big customers were only really valuable customers in the long term, so the expense of recruiting them could only be justified long after they had been incurred. If companies only replaced alarm systems every ten years, you had to have a foot in the door all the time and allow for the fact that you might have to wait for years for the big purchase.

Let's stick with the example, because it shows us what LTV really means. Here we track a single customer –

Customer A	Year 1	Year 2	Year 3	Year 4	Year 5
Goods & services sold	Additional 2 sensors and system check Free survey	Annual system check and maintenance Replacement of 4 sensors	Annual system check and maintenance	Annual system check and maintenance	Annual system check and new alarm system
Invoice value	£ 80	£440	£180	£180	£5380

In this table we show how after being recruited in year 1, the value of Customer A didn't really take off until year 5 when it was clear they needed to upgrade their alarm systems.

Now, suppose in year 1 we had looked at Customer A and tried to assess their profit contribution to our business. We might even have calculated how much it had cost to gain them as a customer.

Customer A	Year 1
Goods & services sold	Free survey Additional 2 sensors and system check
Invoice value	£ 80
Cost of goods sold and engineer's time	£120
Marketing expenditure	£120

Of course these figures are fictional, but they are based on specific components of the service. You'll need to derive your own figures for a similar calculation. Here the engineer's time is costed at £50 an hour and the sensors cost £10 but are charged out at £40 each. The system check is an annual check which takes just 30 minutes (and is usually subject to a minimum call out charge of £80). In this first year, the free survey included the system check and took two hours[5]. Time taken for maintenance can vary but is charged based on engineer's time.

So Customer A, in fact, cost *Gotcha* £160! If we were a short-sighted business we would probably panic as this stage. We'd certainly panic if there was also customer B, C, D, E . . . all the way through to Z. (26 customers × £160 = £4160 lost!).

But this panic should only happen if we really didn't see it coming. If we were able to look at a five or ten year 'history' of such customers, we would have known. And that's why it's so important to keep good records now.

In the next table we look at the same customer and the costs and income over five years:

Customer A	Year 1	Year 2	Year 3	Year 4	Year 5
Goods & services sold	Free survey Additional sensors and system check	Annual system check and maintenance. Replacement of 4 sensors	Annual system check and maintenance	Annual system check and maintenance	Annual system check and new alarm system
Invoice value	£220	£440	£180	£180	£5380
Cost of goods sold and engineer's time	£120	£165	£125	£125	£2020
Marketing expenditure	£120	–	–	–	–

Now we can see that the profit figures look rather better £6400 (invoiced sales) – £2675 (our costs) = £3725 (profit!)[6].

Now it's clear that Customer A came good. They were worth sticking with, weren't they? In fact they turned a profit in year 1, but how could we know that they would be so profitable after four years?

Again the only way of knowing this is in retrospect. No-one can really predict which clients will become the most profitable, but you can develop your hindsight. As we said before, you can and should record everything about your clients so that you *can* look back.

In addition, and just as importantly, you need to give your clients every opportunity to become good customers. In many businesses, after all, just because a customer buys from you once, it doesn't mean they are going to buy from you again, ever. Remember the

Holden-Wilde matrix? Can you make it so that the next time they have to buy they come to you?

For a moment then you might want to think if your business tends to encourage customers to return. Are you the coffee shop that never finds out the names of your regular customers? Some customers want to remain anonymous, and others like to be noticed. What about the hair salon that does nothing to help their clients to make the next appointment while they are still in the salon? Then there is the engineering company that makes a one-off sale for a new customer and never makes a follow-up call to see how things are working.

It's probably, therefore, wrong to leave that last row of the table blank for years 2 to 5. We might take also want to take into account the cost of managing this customer. But how much should we spend and on what?

In a direct marketing approach:

- **Your aims are –**
  - **To keep your customers**
  - **To sell them more**
  - **To sell them complementary products**
- **Your customer's experience is key**
  and
- **Customer satisfaction is not enough**

So the upshot is that you need to monitor your customers and manage them and, crucially, this should be considered an ongoing marketing cost. It's the cost of guaranteeing that ongoing business from someone who *has been* a customer once and *may* come back.

Remember, this customer (a person or a business) has already told you the most important thing about them. They like your product or service enough to buy it once. So will they buy it again?

In the case of *Gotcha*, Customer A in the table was buying a few hours of an engineer's time and a few low-value items.

Now we need to experiment . . . how can we get customers to the point where we guarantee that, like customer A, they will turn into the type of customer in year 5 we love so much?

Now we're looking at customer B –

Customer B	Year 1	Year 2	Year 3	Year 4	Year 5
Goods & Services sold	Additional sensors and system check Free survey	Annual system check and maintenance. Replacement of 4 sensors	Annual system check and maintenance	Annual system check and maintenance	Annual system check and new alarm system
Invoice value	£220	£440	£180	£180	£5380
Cost of goods sold and engineer's time	£120	£165	£125	£125	£2020
Marketing expenditure	£120	£150	£100	£100	£100

– and we've budgeted to spend something each year on keeping them.

The conservative small business will try and save this money rather than investing in their most valuable asset (the customers, as if we need remind you). But bear in mind, if you had **one** customer like A it could pay for **eight** like customer B above to be cultivated. If two of these come good in the same way, you've doubled your profit. But then if you have £100 to spend on keeping each customer happy each year, what *could* you do?

If you're worried that this is too far from a shoestring budget, then think laterally. Investing your time in customer relationships is also a cost but one you tend not to measure so well. If it's your business, call customers personally, get to know them, play golf with them (if you must) but do keep a note of how much you are investing in them – you may be surprised.

Bear in mind also that you can carry out these calculations for groups of customers (segments or clusters) or for different products or services. It then helps you to look at the costs involved in getting and keeping different sorts of business. Too often in small businesses, costs are not attached to individual customers when they should be. A customer worth £20,000 recruited from an exhibition that cost £1000 to attend has to repay that investment.

If you want to explore LTV a little more there is some useful information at the Harvard Business School website and the Database Marketing Institute. The Institute of Direct Marketing also runs short courses on most aspects of direct and relationship marketing[7].

See the free Toolkits on direct marketing (and other useful topics!) online at *www.acblack.com/business.*

Customer service

At its most basic, customer service is about delivering what you promised. Your great ad said that your furniture was solid pine, in a range of styles and at great prices. Is it? When you walk into your own store, do you see the promise being delivered from the first moment?

There are so many examples it's hard to know where to start. So, using the Holden-Wilde matrix...

1. **Selling huge bespoke concrete mixing equipment. The handful of clients in the market for these spend a long time putting together a specification. Given that all**

who tender meet these requirements, they can then make their decision based on price. But you don't want to be in that position. What can you include in your tender that, at any given price, represents added value? *Is it environmentally friendly, is it well-designed, is it easier to clean, do you offer a frequent health and safety check? We're friendly, more flexible. We organise the finance. Every time we finish on site we seed it with native wild flowers.*

2. Selling houses. It's got enough bedrooms, it's in the right place and it's about the right price. But the client usually has to fall in love. So you help the *seller* present their house, you offer 'decluttering' and cleaning services, making every home a show-home. *With our platinum service, we clean and tidy on the Friday and bring fresh flowers then we accompany all viewings over the weekend.*

3. Chimney sweep. The real problem isn't sweeping the chimney; it's remembering to book it and having to be in when it's done. So can you make the appointment for the client, for the same time every year? Can you offer a secure system of neighbour supervision? *We're happy to call round at a neighbour's, or will collect keys from you,, we're police-checked and leave you a written report on the state of your chimney.*

4. Office supplies. They're boring and the client always uses the same supplier, why should they change? They're there on time, we never run out of stock. But what if you can order all your printed stationery in exactly the same way? *We'll hold it in stock and you just order when you need to . . .*

Satisfied customers are not necessarily loyal

Remember in Chapter 3 we mentioned customer satisfaction surveys and above we used a similar scale to rate our service against competitors. That five-point scale from 'disastrous' to 'wonderful' is actually even more significant than we let on.

It so happens that some pretty big companies (and some big-hitting academics[8]) have worked out that the score you get may be worse than you think. They discovered that, in some cases, the 'totally satisfied' customers were six times more likely to repurchase than the merely satisfied. In fact, they say, businesses should focus on those customers who are not *quite* satisfied with the aim of making them into the kind of customer who gives top marks every time – so-called apostles or ambassadors.

Why is it that in some hair salons, you are given a cup of coffee while you wait? If you're in a comparable business, you probably look upon that cup of coffee (and the time taken to prepare it, keeping the coffee fresh and the cups clean) as a cost coming straight out of your profit.

And you'd be right. Except that you've got no figures on the other side; what does that cup of coffee gain you? Remember a cost that doesn't create any value for your business (ie your customers) is an unnecessary cost. So, is there a value to a cup of coffee for your waiting customer?

Yes, because although the coffee itself may cost a few pence (and it really is that little), the preparation and presentation of a cup of coffee has much more cultural significance. It's how you behave towards a friend, or at least a respected acquaintance. If this was your home, you'd look after your guests and it's exactly the same in your workplace. In fact Loaf Hair Salon in Sheffield go even further with wine, beer, a glass of Pimms and even a cocktail of the day[9].

Putting things right

This is our personal plea to all of you to promise to resolve problems that your company creates for your customers. You know the situation, where the meal has to be sent back at the restaurant, a delivery is late and causes major problems for your customer, one of your products damages the property of a customer, etc.

Some of these incidents are covered by insurance policies, but it is the day-to-day (almost minor) problems which concern us most. We believe that most people will accept something going wrong, but it is the way that it is resolved which can help to set your business apart.

A simple example of how not to put it right concerns a store in Kent. When we complained that the cake we had been given was stale, we were given a refund voucher which we had to take to the next floor to a central cashier to claim back our 75p, and we had to queue! We never went back and to this day tell people about their customer service. The solution? Clearly to replace it immediately with a much more expensive item (yes, as much as £1) 'on the house', to show how sorry they were for the mistake.

We would then have told a very different story . . . and put it in the book.

And don't forget that not all of your customers are stupid ... if you're going to serve coffee, you'd better make sure it's the very best cup of coffee you can get because if it's not, your customer probably won't be *totally* satisfied. So maybe instead of paying 30p a cup, you're going to have to lay out 50p a cup and take some care in choosing the coffee machine; not going for the plastic cup, freeze-dried multipack, plug'n'play offer from the vending machine company. You could also follow the lead of retailers in Buenos Aires who find a local café to supply all of their drinks, who after all are specialists, and deliver a better cup of coffee than you can make yourself.

In short, do what you can to *delight* that customer because he or she represents money now and money in the future. And every retained customer is another one you won't have to spend marketing money on recruiting in the future.

Can you relate to poor customer service?

You can see what a tyrant *really* excellent customer service can be.

Here is a test for you. List five examples of outstanding customer service that you and your family and friends have enjoyed in the last year, and then list five examples of poor service. This is a typical exercise in marketing training and most people can list negative experiences but very rarely positive experiences.

It is very often small businesses which are renowned for their approach to customer service: and this can often be a source of competitive advantage. There are, however, clear opportunities to take customer service to the next level.

Moments of Truth

We frequently talk about how we need to see our business from the point of view of the customer, but how do we know how they feel when they buy from us, or attempt to buy from us?

A very useful exercise to undertake is to consider the idea of 'Moments of Truth'[10], which considers **when** a customer is likely to judge our approach to customer service. While this will highlight the things that our customers do value, it will also point out areas where we need to improve. These moments of truth are occasions that a customer comes into contact with our business and what they experience at each point of contact. This is clearly something that you should do for your business. We will look at two examples of a mainly positive experience, and one where it is a very poor experience for a customer.

Booking into a hotel

Based on many years of staying in hotels and a friend who is an international hotel inspector, we present the stages that customers go through when staying in a hotel.

Moments of Truth	What they mean to the customer
You phone the hotel, they offer you a price in line with your expectations. You agree to book a room.	*This is very encouraging and has saved you the time of having to compare lots of hotels and rates online as you are booking at the last minute.*
The booking process is smooth, and they process your details quickly through their software that replicates data from your postcode. They make a note of your special request for a balcony.	*This is reassuring and they are taking care of some of the things that usually cause you anxiety on trips.*

Moments of Truth	What they mean to the customer
You receive an e-mail confirming the reservation, how you will pay and clear directions on how to get to the hotel.	*You have tangible proof of the booking, which is further reassurance for you and means that you have to worry less about the booking.*
You arrive at the hotel by car and a space has been reserved for you.	*You nearly didn't bring the car because parking at hotels has proved to be so problematic in the past.*
The receptionist is friendly, processes your booking quickly, confirms your special request, and points out the services in the hotel lobby. She offers to make a reservation for dinner and book an alarm call.	*The attention to detail makes you feel more relaxed and that you are dealing with very professional people, unlike some of the places you have stayed in.*
You are shown to your room. The room is clean and bright and there is a note welcoming you to the room. The porter quickly shows you round the room, and locates the ironing board and kettle. He also points out that these services can also be booked via room service, and that they have a one-hour turnaround on shirt ironing.	*They are anticipating your needs. Your first call is usually to see if they have an ironing board. When they offer to iron for you usually it takes two days for the ironing to be delivered. This is no good for next day's meeting and on more than one occasion you have had to attend a meeting with a slightly creased shirt, keeping your jacket on in very high temperatures.*

Moments of Truth	What they mean to the customer
The bathroom has complimentary toothpaste and razors.	*This is good to know. Even after years of using hotels for business, you usually manage to forget something.*
You relax and put on the TV and the instructions are clear.	*They have thought about this. You usually have some problems with working the TV in hotel rooms.*
You go to dinner and are welcomed by name. You are offered a chance to sit at a table for the 'Diner's Club' which is for those people who are on their own but who would welcome some company for dinner. You decline.	*They seem very professional and genuinely pleased to see me. You had been thinking of going out but they made it far too easy to book and they sold the menu to you. The Diner's Club might be a good way to network and you will consider it next time.*
At reception you ask for information and they are knowledgeable about the local area. They reconfirm your alarm call even though you don't ask.	*They seem on the ball and aware that you are not from the area and keen that you enjoy your stay.*
As you check out they give you a username and a password to make it easier to book one of their rooms next time.	*This is great. They are going to make it easier for me to book rooms in the future. I will definitely put them in my top three list.*

Before you start e-mailing us and asking for the details of this hotel, we have to point out that it doesn't exist. Although we have no doubt it's described in a corporate manual somewhere...

Buying a computer

Let's look at this from another angle – trying to buy a computer. A typical computer store is out of town, usually very busy at the weekend, and run through a centralised stock system. Most consumers are unlikely to be very knowledgeable about the technical aspects of computers. The shop floor can be daunting, as can their sales staff, who use technical jargon constantly. Even if they sell you a model, it might not be in stock. They offer you no apologies but the chance to come back in your own time to pick it up. No, they won't waive the delivery charge on this occasion. When you do get it home, it inevitably goes wrong and you are passed on to the helpline which you pay for on a premium rate.

All this ties in with some research which looked at the expectations of customers, based on the goods or services that are being purchased[11]. We mentioned earlier the experience of car servicing and all of you who have ever dared to step into a car showroom can relate in some way to the findings. They concluded that customers start with low expectations... and even these are rarely met!

How about...?

Working out what the moments of truth are for your business, using our examples. You should look at this from a customer's point of view and write down all the times that the customer has contact with your business.

If you are going to run a hotel, then stay in one to see how well they do things. Pretend to be on business and request the things that you think should be standard. How do they deal with things that go wrong? If the internet access isn't working then do they have any alternatives?

How well do their staff present the business? If you are going to set up a restaurant, then what kind of experience is it, and what do they promise you?

Our thanks to Gary Cook at BEP Solutions for sharing some of his experiences as a Training Provider frequently staying in hotels all around the UK.

The value of failure

In every service encounter, there is the possibility of failure. There isn't an organisation in the world that doesn't occasionally disappoint a customer. This is the moment of truth *par excellence*. When something goes wrong, you put it right. There is nothing more straightforward or more challenging. It means that the person right there in front of the customer or holding the phone has to be able to act *immediately* for the benefit of the customer.

Look back at the *Gotcha* security example on pages 123–124. Those figures for the ongoing marketing costs to customer B could just as easily be a budgeted figure for your sales people or key account manager. With £100 (figuratively) in their back pocket for the client when things go wrong, what couldn't they do? If you think this is fanciful then think again. We know several small businesses (and one or two large ones) that give everyone in the front line their own budget to spend on customers. It's rapid and flexible, staff just have to report on how it's spent, *afterwards*. The system is … don't let the system get in the way of satisfying customers.

Even if customers leave you, it's still worth keeping in touch with them. They haven't ceased to exist, they've just made a decision. They might come to regret that decision and you should give them reasons to do so as well as plenty of opportunities to return. These kinds of customer are still more valuable and easier to recruit than completely new ones. You'll think about these customers as you work through Chapter 6 since they are the best prospects for generating new business. So if you have list of old customers, use it.

What next?

The message from this chapter is that before you embark on the pursuit of brand new customers, it makes economic sense to spend more time working on the relationships with the customers you already have. You should be able to quantify the value of customers and begin to prioritise them.

We looked at how research will help you to understand this relationship and customers' requirements of you. By simply improving customer service and looking to add value, not only can it increase sales but it might also help you to prevent a future loss in customers and ultimately in revenue.

You should now be aware of the importance of Lifetime Value and the benefits of improving relationships with customers who don't always make frequent purchases. You need to explore how you can add value through extra service and identify your customers' moments of truth with your company.

All this will prepare you for the next chapter where we concentrate on gaining new customers who, of course, you will also want to retain.

Notes/References

1. Brady, N. (2004). 'In search of marketing orientation. An experiment in key account management.' *Market Intelligence & Planning* **22**(2): 144–159.

2. All information concerning individuals collected by a company is subject to data protection legislation. You can find guidance on this at the Information Commissioner's Office website (*www.ico.gov.uk*). Incidentally, this is not something that can be ignored – **all** organisations, no matter how small, must register and can be fined if they fail in their duties under the regulations.

3. *http://smallbusiness.officeline.com* from Microsoft which contains some useful information as well as links to software.

4. Hey! You're a customer on the top left of the Holden-Wilde matrix. It's expensive and troublesome; it's certainly high involvement, you won't make this purchase very often. Now, how do all those computer companies help you out?

5. Those of you who are extremely picky, or smart, might point out that the engineer is charged out at £50, but we don't say how much he or she costs. Well, the point is that our engineers are salaried so they represent a fixed cost – they cost the same no matter how many hours they work. That makes it difficult to allocate these to individual customers. Nevertheless we should try – but it can only be an estimate.

6. OK, OK. Let's deal with it. Someone is asking about the difference between gross and net profit, and do the figures take into account overheads? Well we've already said that the engineer's time doesn't show any profit on a job-by-job basis; our aim therefore is to book out as many hours as our engineers have. We can do a quick calculation to work out the break-even number of hours – how many we have to sell per month or per year to pay for the engineers.

We could do the same for any other costs that are, in fact, overheads – the costs of running the office, etc. But crucially, these can't be allocated to individual jobs. Instead we can look at the profit per job above, and treat it as gross. Then gross profit here is seen as a contribution to overheads.

Also important, is that if we bill NO jobs in a month these overheads still have to be paid. So if those overheads (other than engineers) amount to, say, £700 a month then that is the break-even figure for gross profit on jobs invoiced; only after you cover this do you start to make real profit. Clear? Good.

7. The Lifetime Value resource is at *http://hbswk.hbs.edu/ archive/1436.html* and another similar resource is at *http://www.dbmarketing.com/special_ltv. htm*. Both are in dollars and take some work to understand, but they are easy to adapt to your own needs.

8. Jones, Thomas O. and Sasser Jnr, W. Earl (1995). 'Why Satisfied Customers Defect', Harvard Business Review, Nov/Dec.

9. *www.Loafhair.com*, as featured on Channel 4's *Risking It All* TV programme.

10. Carlzon, J. (1987). *Moments of Truth*, Ballinger Publishing Company, Massachusetts.

11. Shaw and Ivens (2005), The Marketing Forum.

6 GETTING NEW CUSTOMERS

We look at the ways of attracting new customers to your business within a pre-determined budget, using your existing customer base to help target similar types of customer.

We add to the direct methods already described dealing with low-cost ways of communicating with potential customers and so generating sales. We also introduce you to the importance of branding as the basis of consistent marketing communications.

So, how do I get new customers?

The first stage in using a direct approach to gain new customers is … to look at your existing customers. Really look at them. It's called profiling. So re-read Chapters 2 and 3 and remind yourself what you know about your best customers (that's their profile) and, from Chapter 5, what you are doing to keep them and grow them.

As a result of knowing your customers, you will have at least one (and possibly two, three or more) 'clusters' of the kind of people (or companies) you serve. These are your guides to finding new customers.

Many marketing books will ask you to consider a circular target with your customers at the centre. The problem with this image is that you may have several customers in different places, so each represents a different kind of target. In any case, what do the outer rings really mean? Should you be happy if you pick up customers who are 'off target'? For large companies with a wider margin for error, the broad target is okay. In truth, most small companies can't afford to hit anything other than the bullseye.

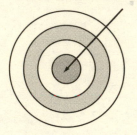

As we said right at the beginning, there are customers out there who are *rightfully* yours and they are the ones you should be aiming at. You should, if you already have (good) customers, be considering how you go about targeting others who are *exactly like them*. We think it's more useful to think of your actual customers as being a very small cluster of customers (in a big market) right at the top of a pyramid (see the diagram opposite).

The key principle

The whole aim of this chapter then is to prompt you to start acquiring new customers with the *most* direct methods possible. Only when you cannot meet your objectives in this way do you then consider more 'distant' methods – even here you will encourage close interaction. Later, if you can afford it, you may use other methods to help 'warm up' the market. But to start with, you should start at the top of the pyramid; we'll come to the labels on the diagram later.

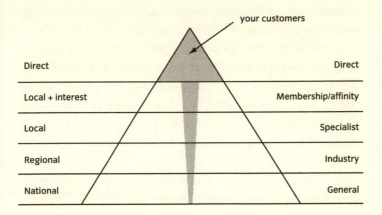

One customer at a time

Remember, really small companies are aiming at getting one customer at a time – and quite rightly. It's expensive to gain a customer and it's just as expensive to serve that customer. So if you break the bank recruiting one customer (from the wrong place) who turns out to be difficult to satisfy (because, in truth, you can't possibly do everything they want you to), then you'll really suffer. To help you think about targeting your ideal new customers, you need to think about the 'channels' you could use to communicate with them.

Right at the top of the pyramid are your customers (of course, you don't have them *all* as your customers yet . . . but give it time). These are the people that you should be talking to as if they *are* customers, even if they are not. Look back at your customer service ideas developed in Chapter 5.

Companies who give information out as part of their service can do this easily. The marginal additional cost of sending your customer newsletter to people you really *want* to be your customer is minimal. If you usually speak directly to your existing customers (and you should), then you should do the same with prospective customers who fit the right profile.

So, at the top of the pyramid you use the most direct, targeted 'channel' possible. Everyone you address here is either a customer or a potential customer with a proven need for your product and so there is no wastage. You MUST consider talking face-to-face, using the telephone or, occasionally, writing personal letters as your primary forms of communication. On a shoestring, there is no substitute; it is the most effective.

If, as a result of the research work you've done (in Chapter 3), you now know the names and addresses of very high-value potential customers, then you should be looking after them very well – directly. Don't waste time finding clever ways to reach them . . . call them now.

Of course, if you're dealing with a large number of customers (of smaller value) and are unable to deal with them all individually, you still need to look after them, but much more efficiently – perhaps online, perhaps simply encouraging them to visit your store. It's in these parts of the Holden-Wilde matrix that you may need to use more conventional 'marketing communications' channels.

Let's make this very clear. If you know who your customers are and who should be your customers; you know their names and where they are, *and* that the total number you can identify more than meets your objectives, then you *do not need* to consider any further 'customer acquisition strategy' such as advertising or PR.

How about . . .?

Talking directly to potential customers. If you wanted to talk to the people who were buying interactive kiosks for stores, airports and other situations, for example, you'd have to visit KioskCom, the two-day exhibition at London's Olympia.

Make sure you go with plenty of your business cards and brochures, if you have them. Visit the stands that offer what you offer and stand alongside customers as they enquire. Chat to people. Ask them what they think of the competitors on view.

For most business-to-business exhibitions, you don't have to pay to visit – and you get around a lot more than if you buy a stand.

If you decide to invest some money, think about volunteering to run a conference session, where you'll be talking to a sub-set of exhibition visitors who are really interested in what you have to say; they're right at the top of your 'customer pyramid'.

Going further afield?

If you find that you can't reach your objectives just from the potential customers you can contact directly – if you are on the right-hand side of the matrix – then you will have to look further.

This is when a wider range of communications activities might be employed. You're looking further down the pyramid, trying to get 'your' kind of customer to identify themselves – so-called 'hand waving'.

Now look back at the labels on the pyramid diagram on page 143. On the left of the pyramid are the kinds of media you might use for attracting individual customers, while on the right are those you might use for company customers, but these are not firm rules.

What is clear though is that, as you move down the pyramid, the customers available out there are few and far between, at least in relation to all the people and companies that you *can* contact. Hence the narrowing 'stripe' of customers shown in the pyramid diagram[1].

The point here is that in order to acquire customers through the usual media (TV, radio, even local or specialised press) you have to be extremely careful about selection. As you move down the pyramid there are greater and greater 'audiences' – clearly the national media (or, on the other side, general business journals) have wide readership – however they will probably not yield a very high percentage of your ideal customers.

To put it another way, in order to 'buy' 100 potential customers towards the bottom of the pyramid, you would have to also buy a greater number of non-customers. It's pretty obvious that if your customers come from your immediate locality, then local media makes more sense. But you can refine this even further, since you might also, for example, find a local newsletter or club for avid book readers or for engineering businesses. If there isn't one, you might create one to begin this form of 'affinity' marketing. It's simply looking for suitable 'clusters' of customers that already exist and improving your strike rate. Increasingly, these kinds of subgroups are represented online – groups on Facebook are worth investigating.[2]

To affinity and beyond

Of course, there doesn't need to be a very immediate link between a cluster of customers and your product or service. You could get the same benefits of so-called 'affinity marketing' through developing a new variant of your product or service.

How about...?

Taking your product or service to new customers. Perhaps what is stopping people from buying is that they haven't sampled the product. In this case, shouldn't you be taking it directly to potential customers?

If your baked bread is out of this world or your car cleaning system the best, then find ways of showing them off to clusters of potential customers. Farmers' markets are great examples of this.

Can you work in partnership with other local businesses? A number of English vineyards we have visited use sampling very effectively as a selling tool!

For example, it may be possible to develop a version of your service just for the local football club and its supporters or for the primary schools in your area. It may have to include a different kind of pricing or a personalised service of some kind and it will certainly include a different form of communication.

If you had, for example, a dry cleaning service which fitted the needs of a local sports team, you could perhaps offer a very low-cost service to the club in return for access to their supporters. It could, indeed, be part of the deal that supporters paid the standard price but some of that went into club funds. In effect the club's supporters become *your* 'members' too and you might recognise this with a membership card – if it's affordable.

Further down the pyramid you begin to use the more conventional media. In each case you need to look at its *efficiency* in reaching your exact audience. Don't be swayed by the idea that seeing your company name in a paper or magazine you read is good publicity; it's only good if it gets you enough customers.

Many of the techniques in this chapter can be used at any level of the targeting pyramid. It's up to you to check and check again that the ones you choose are the most effective and, as a guide, the nearer they are to your customers at the top, the better. You allocate your budget first to the cheapest customers to acquire (ie those most likely to buy) and build up to the more expensive ones.

From prospect to order

Crucially it's not so much the cost of speaking to people that's at issue; it is the cost of turning these into orders that matters. So reaching 400,000 people (on the radio, say) and converting 0.1% is not as good as reaching 50,000 (perhaps in a specialist magazine such as *Practical Boat Owner*) and converting 10%.

Set some goals

At this stage you might set out a range of goals, in the same way that you might look at a range of 'scenarios' as far as your potential market size is concerned (see Chapter 3).

Bearing in mind what we have already said about objectives, you should be very clear about what kind of customers you want (and therefore what constitutes success) and how long you have given yourself to achieve this (and therefore when warning bells might sound if you fall short).

So you might end up with several possible objectives that look like the following (these are clearly written for three different businesses):

- **Gain 1,000 new customers, each spending £1,200 per year, within 12 months**
- **Gain 250 new Gold Card members visiting once a week by the end of the year**
- **Gain six new clients like G. Willing & Son in the next six months**

Now instantly one of the above might leap out as being close to realistic for the kind of business you're running. Your intuition (or your natural optimism or pessimism) may tell you what is possible.

What would be your ideal/realistic objective for a campaign?

In direct marketing the best guide is your experience from past activities. If your monthly advert generates 20 responses, then it's likely to do so in the future. If your mail shot of 1,000 generates 40 enquiries, then you'd expect it to do so again.

However, it's slightly more complicated, of course. The magazine might change or you may use a different list to mail to each month, so you probably ought to budget to be slightly less successful than before. You'd also be well advised to think about what you would do if your campaign was much *more* successful than you expected – could you cope?

But this is only a start, because you also need to set a budget and the budget must fit with the likely success of the project. Even if you are working on a real shoestring at this stage, you will still incur costs (even if it's only paper, envelopes and postage) so you should go through the same process.

Set a budget

The budget must be looked upon as an investment. In direct marketing terms, we need to know the 'allowable marketing cost' (AMC). In this case, that's the cost of acquisition (costs of all the activities needed to secure the customers) that needs to be covered by the increased profit from those customers.

The AMC towards the bottom of the pyramid may need to be higher because it will be more expensive to recruit from these wider, less targeted, 'pools' of potential customers. But you can easily test this.

Allowable marketing cost

AMC or cost per order (CPO) is just a way of thinking about how much you can afford to spend to gain each customer.

Track the value of each customer, then deduct the cost of serving that customer AND any profit you need to make.

It gives you a realistic start point for the cost of recruiting a single customer.

It works like this:		
Selling price		£100
Cost of product	£25	
Order processing etc	£15	
Packing and delivery	£5	
less Total Costs		£45
equals Contribution		£55
Profit required		£40
Allowable marketing cost-per-sale		£15

To put it the other way around, it makes sense that your budget should be spent first towards the top of the pyramid – acquiring the cheapest and more profitable customers first.

Testing an insertion of the same ad or mailing the same number of letters and leaflets to different groups of customers and measuring the results tells you a great deal. How much does it cost to get a customer from list A compared with list B? Or from magazine C compared with magazine D?

It often makes sense to work out AMC on an individual basis – how much can/do you spend to acquire one customer of average value?

Of course you have to spend the money before you get the return. So you would be right to err on the side of caution. You might, for example, decide that in the first instance, you want a return on your investment over two years.

Now you have a measure of efficiency that you can use forever. And if you know you *can* generate customers at £10 or £1,000 each, and you also know how profitable they are, you have a great

151

story for the investor who's going to finance your expansion and a great basis for future marketing budgets.

What we are doing here is the essence of a direct marketing approach[3]. You have to look at the real value of customers over a longer period than just a financial year. Look back at Chapter 5.

Lifetime value (LTV) shows us that some customers are more valuable than others *over the longer term*. Imagine you're promoting your gym. There will be plenty of people who join and who don't renew after their first year's membership has run out. The people you really want more of are those who will join and take extra classes *and* renew. But you can only identify them from looking at existing customers for at least a year and a bit. You want those with the greater LTV.

How about . . .?

Getting your customers to sell for you? For some businesses the best and cheapest way to recruit new customers is by word of mouth. It's often seen as cheap – virtually free.

In fact, to make it work, you might have to give your customers a nudge.

Offering an incentive is quite easy – '10% off your order when you introduce a friend' – but sometimes can appear crude, especially if price is not a primary concern of these loyal customers.

Better still is to offer a free product that is seen as a gift – and share the benefits so that the newly introduced customer gets a gift too.

It can work in business-to-business situations too, but be very wary – some companies don't like their employees to receive personal gifts for spending company money! In this instance a straight discount is often simpler.

Importantly, this applies to *any* business. Even if you see customers only briefly, a single transaction at a time, you should be following the advice in Chapter 5 to develop a relationship. The most valuable customers are not those who give you a little profit once and never return; they are the customers who repeatedly give you profit – and that might take some time.

You'll have to think about this for a while. Taking the third of the objectives we set out earlier as an example, it means that you want to gain six new customers (profiled, remember, like G. Willing & Son on page 149) and may do so within six months, but that they may not become as profitable as you want them to be for two years. Unfortunately it's also difficult to know if you've succeeded for quite a while.

In this example, you will have spent the money long before you get it back and so you might want to allow yourself an additional margin to cover the cost of having that money tied up. So 12 such customers (recruited at **half** the price) might be more sustainable.

This is really comparing your investment in your own business with the alternative . . . like putting it in a bank account. Strange as this may seem, this is the actual comparison direct marketing requires. It's also like the question any investor in your business might ask: does my money work harder invested in acquiring new customers for this business, or on deposit?

So we have to get your investment back *plus*, say, 7% per annum. This kind of sum can also account for inflation – the money you get back in three years may not be as valuable as money today.

These figures can then all be fed into the LTV calculation you've done for existing customers. Remember you had a table similar to the one below for *Gotcha* (the security firm). This one is for *Gutsy* (the gym) and deals with average figures for members, in this case a Gold Card holder.

Gold Card membership	Year 1	Year 2	Year 3	Year 4	Year 5
			Average values		
Joining fee	£30				
Annual fee	£120	£120	£80	£40	£0
Additional classes (average)	£10	£12	£12	£12	£0
Fixed costs/ overheads	£40	£40	£40	£40	
Marketing expenditure	£120	£20	£20	£20	£20
Net income	£0	£72	£32	(£8)	(£60)

The marketing expenditure in year 1 is the maximum 'allowable marketing cost' you chose to set; you didn't want to make a loss in the first year. It could have been more, on the basis that you were confident of keeping this customer for a further two years.

Clearly *Gutsy* isn't in the best of health. Its figures show that Gold Card customers only last four years and their average 'spend' declines. The reason the annual fee goes down in year 4, for example, may be that half of these Gold Card members don't renew and by year 5 they've all left.

Having read Chapter 5, you should have some ideas about what the gym owner can do to retain and grow customers. As far as recruitment is concerned however, he or she should be looking to acquire customers at a lower cost per order so that they become more profitable earlier. What if it only costs £80 to get each customer?

Check it's realistic

Of course if you have never tried this before, your estimate of the number of customers you can gain and how much they are worth might be wrong. In fact, it's actually more likely that you are wrong than right. But direct marketing is, at least partly, about learning (if you want to be smart, you can call it 'continuous live testing'). So before we go any further, we need to make sure we will learn from our mistakes (or our stunning success).

Record everything

It can't be over emphasised in direct marketing how important it is to keep very good records. Having a file where you note down all your decisions, the costs attached to these and copies of every document, is vital.

Don't fall into the trap of kidding yourself a campaign has been successful because you got one or two potentially huge customers 'expressing interest'. At this stage of the game you have to be hard on yourself (and others). Prospects are only customers when they've paid you. Why didn't the campaign 'deliver' when it was supposed to? Did anything go wrong? And if it did, what difference did it make?

How about?

Keeping a 'guardbook'. It's just a direct marketer's term for a file for each campaign.

Every campaign and every activity within a campaign, no matter how small, should be recorded.

Give each activity a title that means something to you and record EVERY expense and EVERY decision. Even down to the typefaces used, the style of the envelope, the day of the week it was sent and received. All of these might be things you could change next time to see if can work better.

If your plan was to get £2,000 of business by the end of March and you have only an appointment with a 'prospect' on the 31st, then your campaign has failed – at that point. But it's important you keep tracking the campaign even after the initial deadline has passed, since you might find it simply takes longer than you expected. Don't be like some companies and forget the campaign as soon as it has finished; we've known of responses coming through a few months after a campaign has ended and going un-noticed; so the campaign was regarded as a failure.

In order to track you must somehow *always* ask the question 'where did you hear of us', or have some kind of coded response device like a coupon or a dedicated phone number and *record the response*.

It's worth repeating this to everyone involved – **track everything, always.**

What to do with failure

Failure is OK. If you've kept your records, you should be able to see at a glance the extent of your failure. You may have spent £1,000 on a simple mailing campaign and gained £200 worth of business. Not good, but then at least you have information and you need to spend some time investigating that.

Let's imagine the £200 came from three small customers. These are now very important to you, not just because they represent your £1,000 investment, but because they may give you clues to other, similar, potential customers.

Your customer acquisition campaign doesn't end when a customers buys. There are now four things you need to do.

1. **Look after these new customers, of course.**
2. **Find out as much as you can about them.**
3. **Find more of them.**
4. **See if you could recruit more, more cost-effectively.**

Look after your customers

It stands to reason that if you've spent £1,200 to get three customers and they've spent a total of just £600 so far, you need to get more out of them. Keep looking at those figures: £400 per new customer who's spent just £200 – the numbers should be seared into your brain!

Call them, meet with them, and find out what else you can do for them – remember, they cost you at least £200 each (£400 minus £200). Wouldn't it be great to turn these customers into profit? As we've said in Chapter 5, looking after the customers you have is often more important than finding new ones. But if you can turn them into, say, £800 clients then you now know these kind of customers are worth targeting in the future.

Find out more about them

As you're talking to these new customers, what else can you discover? Where are they? What do they do? How big are they? Why did they respond? What else do they buy?

You may find that these customers also buy products that are complementary to those purchased from you. One company we worked with was selling basic food products into commercial kitchens, but these clients were buying hundreds of other items from other suppliers such as prepared products and utensils and were concerned about food hygiene issues.

You have an important (strategic) decision to make!

If you already provide the complementary product, then perhaps you can include this in your offer; if you don't, perhaps you should? It's a strategic decision because it could change the whole direction of your business. The food business company also became a food preparation company *and* an education and training company to meet more of the needs of its customers, thus increasing their value.

Do it cost effectively

Go back to your records. The cost of your campaign was relatively high. What could be done more cheaply? Remember, you kept a note of everything so consider what would happen if you used a cheaper envelope? If you used a smaller type size, would the pack be smaller? When postal rates changed in the UK, some companies realised that they could save money simply by using a smaller envelope, which involved simply folding their existing literature!

How about...?

Lurking! Products like music and software are now very well represented in online communities, but equally groups exist for foodies, engineers, language students and countless other interests. Lurking means that you go and register as a fellow enthusiast on one of the many discussion boards and chat rooms and simply observe.

At first you might just look around and learn (some useful research has been done this way). You can, if you want, introduce new topics of discussion and invite comment on your (or your competitors') product. But take care since the most active online participants are likely to be sticklers for 'netiquette' – the rules that govern their discussions. It's better to be upfront about your position and enter into a genuine dialogue to get the community on your side than to try and promote your product surreptitiously and risk being found out and hounded off the forum – 'flamed', in other words!

> If you want a presence online (to invite the discussion group back to your place!) there is nothing easier than getting free web space with a provider like Google or Myspace.com. Both these also have easy ways of creating you the look of a 'mini site' through Google pages or through Mygen.

But there's also more information that could have strategic importance. Remember you looked after the new customers and perhaps some of them did buy more. So you now have two or more clusters or segments (groups of customers who share characteristics).

Both segments were recruited in the same way but one group only bought the initial £200-worth of product (let's call them 'careful buyers') while the second bought £350-worth over the following year (call them 'keen buyers').

So now your aim is to find more. Since it costs you the same to recruit 'keen buyers' as it does to recruit 'careful buyers' then you know who you should be aiming at[4]. It would be very useful to find out the difference between the two, but you don't want to spend excessively on research (you'd have to add that to the costs of acquiring or serving these customers wouldn't you?).

A table or spreadsheet like the one on page 124 for *Gotcha* would help you to plan how you could recruit more 'keen buyers' – and how much you should, and could, spend. You should be constantly testing and trying to improve your efficiency.

Again, there may be something in the data you already have that would give you a clue.

What to track

Direct marketing convention suggests that you should take into account:

- **Recency** – *how long ago the customer last bought*
- **Frequency** – *how often and regularly they purchase*
- **Value** – *how much they spend*
- **Product category** – *which products*
- **Source** – *how we acquired the customer*

Recency is important because the long experience of many direct marketers is that, all things being equal, your most recent customers are your best. Newer customers are more likely to repurchase than a so called 'lapsed' customer who hasn't bought from you for some time. However, it's worth pointing out that a lapsed customer is still more likely to repurchase from you than a complete stranger – a *potential* customer. They are still at the top of the pyramid on page 143.

In the same way, more frequent customers are more committed to your company or product than those who buy less often. They are also, quite obviously, likely to have a greater need of your product or service. It's quite likely too that they are more valuable customers.

At the same time, customers who buy your most valuable (for that read, most profitable) products are clearly more important than those who buy cheaper, or less profitable, products.

Of course you can immediately see that value and frequency may be linked. You must balance the frequent low-value customer against the infrequent high-value one. It would be useful to plot them on the Holden–Wilde matrix and take into account the costs of servicing such clients.

If you have several products or services, you should also take into account which are bought and by whom. This might be particularly important if, for example, you know that purchase of one product is likely to lead onto another. Or you may have a product that is strategically important, perhaps because you see it as becoming more important over the years. Clearly consumable products run out, so replacement and re-ordering services are useful, particularly if the product is of critical importance to your customer.

Finally, and most importantly, you need to track where customers come from. This is the clue to where there might be more similar customers. Whichever mailing list, newspaper, radio channel, newsletter, event (the list is endless) produces your best customer is worth revisiting.

A commercial photographer we know very often finds new clients when they make a 'distress purchase' – they have been let down by another studio or they have a last-minute requirement that their regular suppliers cannot fulfil. In these circumstances, the work may be very simple and low cost but, as it is an introduction to a new client with frequent photography needs, it's taken very seriously.

A fairly simple scoring system can enable you to make judgements about the kinds of customer you want to keep recruiting. If you're dealing with many customers, the profile (perhaps on a computer system, as in Chapter 5) can include simple 'switches' to select on 'source' and 'recency', etc.

Inevitably, you cannot always log all customers and their visits or enquiries – but you should try to make it part of the company culture. Every communication should have a clear way for potential customers to respond, and you must capture as much as possible. We have a problem with any company that receives a call from a customer and then tells her to phone back later. What if she had just put you into her 'decision set'? Her next phone call might be to a competitor and you've lost the sale. Why? Because your staff don't understand the importance of logging and dealing with all calls; any one of them could be the business equivalent of a lottery win. Cumulatively, they *are* a lottery win.

Making your communications consistent

In our experience one of the key areas where we can make a difference to a small business is in branding.

As far as your existing customers are concerned, this isn't really an issue. They already use you; presumably they like you. For them, their relationship with you is 'the brand'.

But just remember that if people *don't* know you, then the first time they see you is when they make an instant judgement about you. You only have one chance to make a first impression.

It's very easy to think (as we've said before) that you have a great product and you just need to announce it to everyone. That may be so, but you have to be brutally honest with yourself.

Seth Godin (a true guru if ever there was one) says, 'People are selfish, lazy, uninformed and impatient', then adds the rider: 'Start with that and you'll be pleasantly surprised'[5]. So really, why should anyone care about your new business . . . or your old one that's been around for a while?

Branding as a vibe

Pivotal to the major changes in the Watergate Bay Hotel in Cornwall has been the recognition of the value of a strong brand.

Contrary to what much of the literature on branding might suggest, there isn't one simple idea at the heart of the Watergate Bay brand; rather there is a 'cluster' of values, all of which go together. It's much more than a 'badge' on the letterhead and it's derived from the owners' close understanding of the customers.

The business has a culture which is shared with the customers – it's a 'beach vibe', with an appreciation of good food and drink, chic design, enjoyment, exercise and relaxation. The beach and extreme sports are a key part of the Watergate experience, even if some visitors never get their feet wet, and it's a million miles away from the slightly shabby image of the British seaside holiday.

But even this extensive description doesn't encapsulate everything and sometimes it is easier to visualise what fits and what doesn't.

For example, the clothing that the staff wear is an important part of any hotel. Rather than look like every other hotel (with suits or white shirts and blouses and black trousers) the predominantly young people who work in the hotel wear fashionable 'surf wear' which is provided in a commercial deal with White Stuff (*www.whitestuff.com*).

One of the old-school gurus, Theodore Levitt, said marketing is all about differentiation, but more recent research suggests it's not quite as simple as that. It makes a convincing argument to explain why people are *not* waiting with bated breath for your new business or product.

> 'Most of the items in a store are "discretionary spending" for most of us, most of the time. Be it a hardware store, a grocery store, a clothing store, or even a bank. If we buy an item, we use it, eat it, or wear it. But if we don't, usually without realising, we find something else to do with our time and money. We could get our hair cut this week, but often we leave it until next.'[6]

So customers very often don't care. They don't plan and they don't carry round detailed lists of what they want.

This is one reason why we think the Holden-Wilde matrix is useful, because it not only focuses you on how many customers you have – both potential and actual – but also on how 'premeditated' the decision to purchase is. In addition it also gets you thinking about how important the product is; a purchase perceived as expensive by the customer will be given more conscious attention than one that is cheaper and routine.

In the latter circumstances it's likely also that customers will go through a more drawn-out decision making process. This is important. On a limited budget you can only afford to aim at customers who are ready to buy *now*. They are right at the top of the pyramid we looked at earlier.

Hopefully by now time and money spent on making the product or service work and setting the price is seen as an investment, but what about building your brand? What makes a brand even noticed and therefore considered as an option? How do potential customers let you know that they are ready to buy?

How about...?

Telling the truth. It's not that fashionable, but we really believe that your brand has to be truthful.

We don't disagree with Seth Godin but, in fact, as far as promotion is concerned, people aren't stupid.

If your business is called *The 5 Minute Dry Cleaning Co.* and you always take half an hour, then it's telling a lie every time it's seen in public.

Conversely if you've decided, in Chapter 1, what you and your business are all about and you're developing a plan to do exactly what you say you will, then tell the world.

The truth... *that's* your brand.

Sometimes it's in a store or it's in a magazine or a directory; it may be on a high street or at a business exhibition. But you have to be noticed ... and you don't have much time.

It's pretty much true that you have only 5–10 seconds for an advert to catch a person's attention, but a brand has to keep working long after that *and* remember that you're still working on a shoestring. So although you want to grab attention, you can't do that by being loud. You can't have the biggest store or the biggest exhibition stand. You can't afford the biggest space in the fashion buyers' magazine or to flood the directory of office equipment suppliers.

We urge you to think hard about differentiating yourself from the competition. Firstly, if relatively few potential customers see your name, you'd better make sure that when they do, they take notice. It has to say something relevant to them. Secondly, if they do notice you, you have to know what to say. So be clear about the story you are telling (see also the Toolkit: Making an ad at *www.acblack.com/ business*) and always tell the same story. That's your brand.

Branding at its simplest . . .

Mr Locke, the local chimney sweep, like Father Christmas, only visits once a year. But he always tells us when he's coming with a simple card through the door. It's nothing special, just his name and number in neat black print and a space in which the date and time of his annual visit is printed.

The service is great; his customers don't make appointments because he does that for them. He's always on time and scrupulous about keeping his customers' homes clean and tidy – everything is done with military precision but with friendly chat if the client is willing.

The branding? Well, everything about the Mr Locke's service speaks of quiet efficiency with a little bit of *Mary Poppins* tradition: he always wears his top hat.

Some companies, even small ones, feel the need to put a name to every product or service. Hence you have the double whammy of a company you've never heard of and its forgettable products. Ladies and gentlemen, we give you —

Chambull & Snarl's Obfusticator X2020i

— presumably a great advance on the Obfusticator X2020.

It doesn't have to be like that of course. As always, you should think of the customer. A simple name that has the attributes of a strong (and appropriate) brand will always be preferred.

So, if you have a concrete mixer, does it really need a name? For most small companies working on a shoestring it is their relationship with frequent customers that matters, so *that* is what should be promoted. In essence you're saying to the customer, 'We will solve your problem and we'll use whatever equipment is necessary'.

If you only tell customers that you have the Pramac GSL42D generating plant then it's very easy for customers to compare your product with that of the other company down the road, which may offer a better service or a lower price. Never get into the position where you are offering exactly what your competitors are.

As you make decisions about your brand (on a shoestring), you have to question whether you can afford to make both your product name *and* your company name famous. If not, which is the most important?

Turning your name into a brand device

Once you have a name, you have to have a way of presenting it in a consistent and compelling way. But don't finalise the decision on the name until you have at least seen it represented visually.

We hope the company concerned doesn't mind us referring to it, but 'Best Range Labels' probably thought it had a pretty good company/brand name, but they weren't helped by the sign writer who made it look like –

BE STRANGE

You could visit many design consultants and pick their brains. Remember, you're the client so you should never feel obliged to buy. Vision, for example, is a small Brighton-based consultancy that has taken a great marketing approach itself and is giving away valuable information to people like you via its website[7].

For the sake of having a simple rule, here's what we think the brand of your company (and its visual representation) has to do . . .

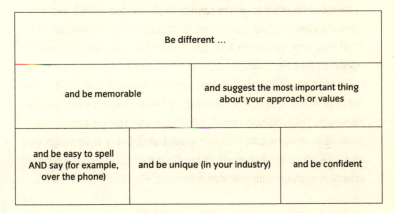

Be different …		
and be memorable	and suggest the most important thing about your approach or values	
and be easy to spell AND say (for example, over the phone)	and be unique (in your industry)	and be confident

It's difficult to say that any of these elements are more important than the others; they all depend upon each other – hence the 'bricks in the wall' of the diagram. If you take one of the elements away, the structure is less sound. Try this test on your competitors.

The key to strong branding thereafter is jealously to guard your brand and ensure that everything you do carries the brand name and the logo in *exactly* the same way. Once you begin to play about with the visual identity of your company, it is irrevocably weakened. So be fussy (no, obsessive) when it's printed in ads, on letters, on the shop front or on t-shirts. If you can't tell that it's exactly right, get other people you trust to point out the flaws and get them corrected.

Advertising and PR can be on a shoestring too

We now want you to consider a range of marketing communications tools as a way of spreading the word about you and your business with the ultimate aim of trying to secure new customers.

Many textbooks are very careful to separate out advertising and PR techniques but our point here is to suggest some strategies for acquiring new customers that are viable for the small business – whatever they are called

As we have said several times, SMEs should be able to identify the type of customers that they would like to attract, and in many situations they actually know the names of the customers they want. But, accepting all that we've said about very tight targeting and efficiency, we still think there is a role for quite traditional advertising and public relations for:

- **establishing contact with potential customers and influencers**
- **maintaining your company's image**
- **keeping the marketplace 'warm'**
- **and ultimately**
- **bringing new customers to you**

How you use these techniques depends to some extent on how many customers there are and how frequently they purchase – points already made since you should, by now, be dreaming about your position on our famous grid! It will also depend on the position of these potential customers on the pyramid we looked at earlier in this chapter.

It pays to network

Samantha Hillas was a solicitor specialising in family law. Samantha was new in Liverpool and was attending business breakfasts as a way of meeting new people in her area. She was also increasingly interested in the field of marketing, and wanted to look at ways of raising the profile of her practice.

At one of the breakfasts she met the business editor of the *Liverpool Echo*, who suggested she write a weekly column covering legal issues.

Samantha's legal practice was very supportive and the minimal outlay every week for the business meetings was never going to break the bank. Samantha was nervous about her first article, but soon got the hang of writing and was thankful for the expert advice of the commissioning editor.

Over time the articles started to pay off for the company, helping to make them better known in a highly competitive marketplace. It became apparent that some of the new enquiries for business were being made as a result of the column. For Samantha herself, the success of the columns may have also contributed to her promotion to the bar.

Press and public relations

Let's take conventional press and public relations – using the media to generate publicity for the company. This is something that all businesses should use, irrespective of size. Public relations (PR) can be used to inform and educate and to begin dialogue with important groups.

Before you start switching off and dismissing public relations as something that isn't for your business, allow us to explain. These techniques are usually within the budget of most small businesses and are relatively straightforward to use. Some of them are more likely to take up your time than your money. Of course time is money, but on small budgets, saving cash may be more important than a night's sleep! So why are these communications techniques important for the small business owner?

The groups you address (who influence your business and your customers to a greater or lesser degree) are often called 'stakeholders'. These include customers but also the local community, your staff, the local council, the local media, suppliers, distributors, industry bodies, the financial community and the media. In fact, anyone who might have an interest in the way your business is being run. We will say more about the media shortly, but needless to say this particular stakeholder is very often the means by which you communicate with the others.

Remember that stakeholders are individuals as well as groups, and you should aim to develop ways of communicating with them that meet *their* communication or information needs. In some cases this might be something as simple as a letter or a personal meeting, but it may mean producing brochures, websites, newsletters or events. If, for example, you need to win over the local council or other 'influencers' then you should address them too.

As we mentioned in Chapter 4, your communications (like any aspect of your marketing) must be adapted to customers and PR is one of the most adaptive approaches of all. It also happens to be the one most easily accomplished on a shoestring.

Let's not underestimate the power of building such stakeholder networks. Networking is vitally important for small business owners, and in particular networking with other business owners. Chambers of Commerce and similar organisations often try and establish 'networking' events, but these are generally selling events and you don't really want to be sold to, do you? There is nothing like having your own network and maintaining it conscientiously.

Why not just advertise?

Our experience of small businesses is that they are often at the mercy of the advertising sales executives of newspapers and local radio stations. Advertising is seen by some as a quick fix and a sure way to get lots of lovely new customers. Why not? The radio ad is heard by 50,000 people and maybe 30,000 people read the local newspaper. But a one-off ad has little impact. The reality is that only a handful of people are likely to react quickly to any advert – it has always been the case. It is too easy to place an advert, hand over the money, get on with the business and believe that you have tried to 'market' the business. But you have to justify this expense in terms of your budgets (see page 150).

Remember, advertising inevitably happens amongst lots of other advertisers trying to do the same thing. By simply looking at your range of stakeholders, you can see that while you *could* pay for advertising to reach them with your messages, there are sometimes more cost-effective ways of doing this. Besides, in most cases, you know who you want to target – refer back to the pyramid.

Consumers often view advertising quite cynically – especially for a company or brand they haven't heard of. Public relations activities can also make people aware of what you do and can work *with* other means of communication to encourage customers to think of you (usually as an authority in your area), put you on their 'shortlist' or to contact you for further information, bringing new prospective customers onto your radar screen. The effect of an apparently non-commercial message is to remove some of the cynicism.

Who needs advertising?

The Watergate Bay resort's full-time marketing director maintains excellent relationships with local and national media and, with a PR agency, works to a carefully worked out calendar of action to keep giving the media reasons to talk about the resort's unique position and offering.

The money the resort used to spend on advertising has been replaced by a PR budget of half that – a sum that can give a lot of journalists a first-hand taste of the Watergate Bay lifestyle.

Barely a week goes by without the resort being mentioned in a national Sunday newspaper.

More recently, the owners gave the media more reasons to notice Watergate when their proposal to locate one of Jamie Oliver's 'Fifteen' restaurants right on the beach was given the green light. It opened in 2006 and has put Watergate even more firmly on the map.

All your marketing expenditure must be accountable so, as you start to plan your public relations activity, it's important to ask yourself what you hope it will add to your business. Even if this is difficult (and it will be), you may still want to proceed knowing that you can gain a great deal of attention for your business or product at very low cost. We are suggesting that public relations should be part of your overheads, that is, the cost of keeping your company or brand in the minds of your customers – but it's still a cost of acquiring and maintaining customers.

Preparing to target stakeholders

Using a grid like the one below, you can start listing the various stakeholder groups in the left hand column, followed by the most appropriate means of communicating with them and finally logging the links that exist with these groups. This becomes part of your marketing information system that will grow as your business does.

For a company supplying the hotel trade with ready-made excursion and information packs, the table might look like this:

Stakeholder/ influencer groups	Most appropriate means of communication (brochure, letter, meeting, newsletter etc)	Current links with stakeholder (identify key people or groups)
Small Hoteliers Trade Association	Meetings Letters Newsletters	Chair person is ... Committee members include ... Other members not known but a list is ...
Tourist boards	Meetings Stand at regional convention	Marketing manager Members
Local tourist information offices	Leaflets Visits (to capture names and introduce service)	Officers

In effect you will be developing a marketing plan for each of your stakeholder groups, except that the product is primarily information and education. Note that the visits in the table aren't used for selling, as such, although this would be your priority.

Using press releases

You use press releases (or news releases) in order to send out information to the press, radio and television when you want them to publicise your business. They can deliver a mass audience to you (the point they will always make to you when they are trying to sell you advertising space) but ... virtually free.

It all sounds very simple and, theoretically, should gain you plenty of articles in the press, coverage on the radio and television and mentions in specialist publications. Unfortunately it's not that simple. The success rate can be low, and that it is all too easy for you to contribute to your own failure! According to experts, as many of 90% of all press and news releases go straight into the bin after the first glance and, of those that remain, a higher percentage go in to the bin after second reading![8] But using our Toolkit for writing a press release (see *www.acblack.com/business*), and bearing in mind the purpose of your business, your brand and your 'truth' you should be able to compile press and news releases.

How about . . .

So now you know what to do, why not start searching for the contact details of the local newspapers, magazines, radio station, TV stations, specialist websites and specialist publications? Sometimes it is worth picking up the phone and speaking to the local newspaper to discuss your story. They will soon tell you if they are busy, but they offer their phone number (in their newspaper and on their website) so you can contact them and feed them interesting news.

One of our clients picked up the phone and had a ten-minute conversation with the local BBC office about how one of his products could help in the fight against childhood obesity. There are usually times to avoid ringing, such as the morning of the print deadline, but you always have the option of sending an e-mail as well.

How can you measure the output of public relations activities?

We've already hinted that you need to consider the value of your public relations activities. If they are an investment, what is the return?

You should be clear that public relations is not just about publicity seeking and, as with all the other marketing tools, you should set clear objectives.

One way of assessing the value of PR output is to measure it in terms of 'advertising equivalency'. If you manage to get a piece on the front page of your local paper, then you can easily calculate the size of the piece and how much that area of the page would cost if you had placed an ad.

Most of the market research activities explored in Chapter 3 can also be used to monitor and measure the effects of public relations activities. If, for example, you were concerned about the perception of your products within the air conditioning industry, then your research might also include asking customers and potential customers (as well as other stakeholders such as journalists) about your image and reputation.

A picture saves a thousand words

In order to support the great story you have developed for your press and news releases, you can also supply photographs and, increasingly, video for use online. These are almost essential since they immediately add impact to your story and present the editor with an additional reason for including it. They also make your item more attractive on a page and more memorable.

An increasing number of companies and their public relations agencies are creating photo opportunities for their stories. There are many examples of organisations setting up mini-demonstrations to make a point to the media, or even creating spoof events. There is considerable expertise needed to make this happen so it could be in your interests at least to consult an agency.

And before you start ordering a fancy dress outfit and parading through your local high street to create 'an event', think carefully about the image you wish to portray. It might not be the best option for the upmarket restaurant/computing/engineering business – well, let's face it, it's probably not right for any business.

The first step is actually to consider the message (remember your insight, your brand) that you want to get across. One of the most striking uses of video is the demonstration of Blendtec® blenders on YouTube. The series of 'Will it blend?' videos perfectly conveys the truth of the brand and has been carried on thousands of web pages and blogs around the world.[9]

Generating leads through sponsorship

There is plenty of research to show that sponsorship is successful, but many writers in this area will now tell you that it can only have an impact on sales if it is co-ordinated with other promotional activities. However, from a small business perspective there are other reasons to invest in sponsorship.

Before you spend money, you should again consider your main stakeholders. Do you sponsor the local football team with a new set of shirts, or would it be better to give up some other resources to help them out. Perhaps you have a spare room on your premises that they could use for club meetings, which would help them to reduce some of their outgoings?

Perhaps your engineering firm would gain more from using its expertise to help a local group, rather than spending £400 on new kit for the under 12s. Could your restaurant be a subsidised venue for the local wine club, or mother and toddler group? Or what about making netball posts for the local women's netball team?

A word of warning. Sponsorship opportunities are often offered to businesses without any concept of the benefits to each party. Always make these decisions with your head – referring back to your strategy. And be careful about sponsoring a sport simply because you enjoy it; there might be a better cause to support. Remember, it only adds value to the business if it adds value *for your customers*. If in doubt, ask your customers; you could even ask them to vote.

The benefits of sponsorship are that it generates considerable goodwill for your company and helps you forge closer links with your community. The estate agent that always sponsors the local primary school fete or the restaurant that provides food for a homeless charity are seen as different *kinds* of business as a result. Of course, as your brand is based on truth it goes without saying that sponsorship agreements shouldn't be taken on lightly – and certainly the negative publicity of suddenly 'dropping' charitable support when the budget is tight needs to be seriously considered.

You will need to set some objectives, such as increased media coverage, improving the reputation of your company, or for example, opportunities to reward your staff and customers with tickets to see the local team that you have sponsored. Working with the local community should help raise the profile of your company and make stakeholders look upon you more favourably but don't be afraid to try to measure this.

Creating events

Events can range from small corporate events consisting of a few clients to large outdoor events organised for the general public. Events can be used to talk directly to customers, staff or indeed most of the stakeholders we have identified in this chapter. But they can also create a wider sense of excitement and interest, enabling customers and others to learn about you.

Crucially such events should be completely in keeping with your brand – your aims and values – a 'brand experience'. A whisky distiller offers places at its 'whisky school'[10] – why isn't there a plumber that offers short evening classes in the local church hall about how to cope in an emergency? Why don't car dealerships offer safety classes for women who drive alone? Events offer a great chance to showcase your business and make people feel as if they know and trust you a little more.

Being a good citizen

The community in which your business operates is a stakeholder too – or rather several thousand stakeholders. Your community is important because it's where your staff live, where neighbours can choose to report if your shop is being burgled and, crucially, where people will complain if they believe your business is irresponsible or undesirable.

Being a good citizen is all about generating goodwill with people who might not be customers, but could be, and who can influence others. It's a mistake to think that the people who walk past your business are 'just' customers (or worse still, unimportant because they're not customers). Indeed the more you have researched them, having read Chapter 3, the more you should be growing to like them. You should certainly take an interest in what matters to them; their community.

What options are there for your business? How closely do you work with the local community? Could you help the local school or college and create some media attention for your business? How about allowing your staff to take some time out every week to help a local charity? This isn't a gimmick to gain short-term publicity, but can be a genuine way to help motivate your staff.

There are numerous opportunities and demonstrating your sense of corporate social responsibility contributes to your business being distinctive and genuinely liked.

Decisions, decisions

You may well be asking, which is the best option for your business?

If in doubt, go back to your earliest decisions. You've decided how many customers you need to gain (and their value) and you know what you have to offer, your brand, your position and how you want your business to be seen.

Your acquisition plan should therefore be based on the most cost-efficient methods of getting this important information to the highest possible number of 'your' customers. This is the only criterion for the choice of communications methods. And remember, the budget has to be allocated in the most efficient way.

You start with the most direct methods. You create opportunities for potential clients to interact with you, by meeting them or giving them the information that they need to make their decision (again as directly as possible). Then you consider more 'distant' methods – always making response as easy as possible. Then, if you can, you may use some of the indirect methods to help warm up the market – to make targeted customers (and influencers/decision makers) more receptive to your message.

The truth

Just a reminder about what should be at the heart of all your marketing activity. The truth is what your customers will find out *after* they have bought from you, perhaps the very first time they use you. And if there is any difference between what you promise and the truth, they will lose faith in you. Eventually they will go elsewhere.

So, make sure you have a 'good truth' to tell, that you always deliver it (that's Chapter 5 in a nutshell) and that your brand image and all your communications always promise it.

What next?

You are now in a position to start putting together your action plan for getting new customers. Remember that in some cases this means stepping outside of your comfort zone and inviting new people in to do business with you.

You will be aware of the need to be realistic in your target setting and to be sure that all of your staff are aware of the implications of trying to attract new business.

Winning a new order and then not being able to fulfil it can send out disastrously negative messages to the market and impact on your ability to win further new business.

You should be building a plan that involves actions focused on the top of your 'customer pyramid' seeking to hit the easiest (and most profitable) targets first. Then you may be working your way down using other, less direct methods helping you establish new contacts, acquire new customers and increase awareness and understanding of your brand among the stakeholders you have identified.

Notes/References

1. In truth, the base of this pyramid could be ten times wider than we show here. The number of 'your' customers out there who are reading or viewing the mass media is tiny. Don't chase big audiences; target your ideal customers as precisely as you can. In the end it's the cheapest way too.

2. For more on this see *Virtually Free Marketing* by Philip R. Holden, published by Bloomsbury Publishing Plc.

3. The Direct Marketing Association (*www.dma.org.uk*) has useful free publications that give you advice on best practice and the rules and

regulations that govern direct marketing. The Direct Marketing Association, DMA House, 70 Margaret Street, London W1W 8SS; tel. +44 (0)20 7291 3300; e-mail *info@dma.org.uk*.

If your business depends on direct marketing, you might find it useful to join the Institute of Direct Marketing (*www.theidm.com*) or go on one of their numerous courses. The Institute of Direct Marketing, 1 Park Road, Teddington, Middlesex TW11 0AR; tel. +44 (0)20 8977 5705; e-mail *enquiries@theidm.com*.

4. Just in case it's not obvious, you should be aiming for more 'keen buyers'. So it's useful to see if there is any obvious difference between the segments you've identified. It could be anything; age, profession, type of company (for company clients) or it might be unknown. In this case, you will have to continue recruiting both, perhaps do some more research, but perhaps also modify the AMC to make the 'careful buyers' a little more profitable.

5. *www.sethgodin.com*

6. Ehrenberg Bass Institute for Marketing Science (*www.marketingscience.info*).

7. Click on Vision's website to see the 'Guide to Branding' and other useful information (*www.brand-vision.co.uk*).

8. David Tebbutt, a respected journalist and trainer in media skills, gives some very handy tips in his interview by Alex Bellinger on the small business podcast (*www.smallbizpod.co.uk*). Other podcasts at the same site are as interesting and useful.

9. Just visit the Youtube site and search for 'Will it Blend?' – I guarantee you'll watch at least three videos and you'll probably tell someone else about these crazy product demonstrations.

10. *www.whisky.co.uk/distillery/whiskyschool.html*

7 KEEPING IT GOING

In our final chapter, we ask you to consider the decisions you've made so far and show you how your plan might look. As you put it into action, we suggest how you can keep it fresh and alive so that you constantly challenge your own assumptions and decisions.

We make a shameless plea to you (and our publishers) for another edition – one in which you might provide the examples. And we reveal the dark secret at the heart of marketing.

Marketing isn't a one-time fix

You may have spent a long time on this book and the work we've given you, but you'll spend less and less time on it as your plans swing into action. Careful. Don't lose sight of the great things you've learned (that in fact, we would argue, you've taught yourself) as you've gone through this process:

- **your vision, your business, the brand that is uniquely yours**
- **your insight into the market, who the customers are and what they need and want**
- **your sense of direction**

- **your marketing objectives – the ones you worked out and prioritised; keeping and growing customers and/ or gaining new ones**
- **your strategy – your unique way of achieving your objectives that will reinforce your values**
- **the great ideas you had to make the strategy real through recognising customers' needs and their cost, convenience and your communication with them**
- **the commitment that you've made to see these plans through**

So keep an eye on these things.

Strangely, you should start at the bottom of the list and refer up. The last question is really about the execution of the plans (did I do what I said I had to?), then up to the plans themselves (were they right, were they realistic?), then your strategic 'direction' (did I research thoroughly?), then your objectives.

But most of all, refer up to your clear statement of values – the things that you really care about. If you're no longer in business for the same reasons, then you need to rethink your values. If the business is growing and it's making money but you're not happy, why might that be? And what can you do about it? Another hairy potato anyone? (Look back at page 19 ... as if you've forgotten!)

Your plan into action

If you've been following the previous chapters closely and actually applying what you've learnt, then you *should* have made some progress. We hope you've tried to work with the simplified strategic tools we've suggested and produced your own plan.

Let's repeat what we said earlier, there isn't ONE plan that will suit all businesses. What you should have is a plan developed by you (and your co-owners and staff) that reflects *your* unique position in *your* marketplace.

Your plan should start off with a clear statement of your values or your aims; the reason why you are in business and why you are different. With luck, you will have described your market in a way that none of your competitors have and you will have a unique view of the direction in which you need to go and how you're going to get there – your marketing strategy.

It's more than likely that you have been back and forth over this process, balancing your own ambitions and abilities with the insight into your customers produced by your research – at least we hope so.

You may have produced some kind of diagram like this:

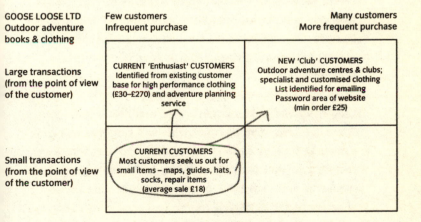

It shows you how you have identified current customers from whom you can get more (sales and profit) and, perhaps, identifies new clusters of customers you feel ideally suited to serve. These are customer groups you feel you 'deserve' more than the competition.

Against each of these, you will have developed plans to acquire them, keep them and grow them.

Current customers: We will continue to serve our current customers in the store. However, making the store more efficient with less floor space given over to stock and more to display (new cabinets and shelving to be installed in June) should enable us to release upper sales floor for the high-performance clothing and café . . .

Enthusiast customers: In our current customer base there are currently 270 such customers to whom we will give free membership to the 'Explorer Café' (with our independent travel planning consultant) on the first floor. We will aim to recruit an additional 50 members this year. These customers currently yield £390 pa and we aim to increase this to £470 pa (additional turnover of £26,000 pa) . . .

Club customers: We currently have eight local clubs to which we give 15% discount. This will continue but a campaign through e-mail lists and online forums aims to recruit a further 20 nationally, to which we will give access to our 'club only' online catalogue. This shows shop prices and a 10% discount. A minimum order level is set . . .

Of course, your plan will show even more detail than this, with very clear measurable objectives shown along with your expenditure and timings of all activities. As you put your plan into action, there will naturally be moments of doubt when you think that maybe this book wasn't worth the money. Relax. Go back through the early chapters again. Remember marketing is about *your* approach to business, and we've tried to encourage you to take an intelligent, insightful and analytical approach.

And remember, this is marketing on a shoestring. The majority of decisions you have taken have involved time, more than money, to get right. You might have invested in:

- **research to find out more about your customers**
- **product development to meet the identified needs of your customers**
- **improved communications with customers and prospective customers**

These things shouldn't be wasted. In fact the last item especially should be paying dividends – as long as you are listening as well as talking.

If you've also managed to get a better grip on your costs and pricing, then you should have a very clear idea (built into your strategy, of course) of where your profit comes from (which customers) and therefore (along with your research) an idea of the size to which your business could grow.

Review progress every day

If you've done as we suggested, then those measurable objectives – which you may also have broken down into sub-objectives or milestones – should be able to be ticked-off on the way.

If your plan covers one year and you are three months in and haven't sold a thing, then look back at the plan. Re-read your explanation of the objective and ask yourself if you had, say, a three-month target. Did anyone else (like the bank manager, your fellow directors or family) expect you to hit particular figures at this time?

You should look at the detailed activities in your plan, whether they are for cultivating your existing customers or gaining new ones. Have they all gone to schedule? Has everything happened as you planned it? For example, you may have produced 10,000 leaflets to attract customers to your gallery, but were they distributed to the right places? Were they distributed at all? Might you have boxes of them sitting in a storeroom 'just in case'? If so, get moving! Any promotional material that's not out there is dead money.

Similarly, if you took delivery of your leaflets late, does that mean everything else in your plan has been pushed back? Timing is critical. In one business we know, summer holiday plans meant that the MD wasn't there to give the final approval to a brochure for a new product launch. The delay of just a few days meant the mailing was delayed even more (as the company handling the mailing had other work on). The result was that the product was barely launched in time for Christmas and vital weeks' worth of orders were missed. The budget for the year then was wildly out.

If you've taken the direct marketing approach to heart, you might also have worked out some interim or indicative measurements you could take into account. For example, you should have built into your communications with consumers some kind of predicted response. Perhaps prospects (potential customers) have to send for a catalogue first before they order? In that case, having figures for the number of catalogues requested may give you an indication of possible orders.

Just a note – even if this is your first campaign, these numbers are important. Remember, *everything* about your best campaign (and your first will be your best, so far . . .) is useful to know. This sets the benchmark for your next campaign.

It's all going horribly wrong

Of course, it's possible that the wheels will fall off your business completely. It happens.

Research into the failure of firms identifies the importance of the resources at the outset – but, crucially, not just financial resources. Of course it can be a struggle to get a small business off the ground and it takes many years (if it happens at all) before a business owner can say that her company is stable.

Many companies fail (and most do so, as we've said, in the first couple of years) because of the innate ability of the entrepreneur. It has been said that the limiting factor to a small company's growth is just that – the owner/manager[1]. But it's also worth reminding yourself that deciding to shut up shop is not necessarily a failure. When you decide that the risks are too great and the rewards too slim, then closing is a victory for common sense.

One entrepreneur friend, from whom we learned much, used to insist on always knowing the 'shutters-down' position, that is, the financial situation you would face if the business closed today.

It isn't quite like the neat figure on the accountant's balance sheet, although it involves totalling all assets and liabilities. In this case it also involves taking a realistic view of the likelihood of getting paid once you announce you are closing (which may include discounting some of your outstanding invoices to get the money in) and accounting for any redundancy payments you have to make or penalty clauses in lease agreements.

Incidentally, don't underestimate the value of the customers you have – you may be able to ease the transition for your customers if you sell the list to another company, perhaps a competitor. At least, armed with the knowledge of the actual value of your business, if you have to make the decision, you can make it fully aware of the size of your loss, or your gain.

Such decision making is when business becomes tough and you realise why so many companies fail even to start the business they plan and, perhaps, why you paid yourself more than the people who seemed to work so hard *for* you. It also takes you straight back to the decisions you mapped out in Chapter 1. Very often in times of stress the realisation dawns, 'This isn't why I went into business'.

It's been said that urgent decisions are generally the wrong ones. It's the difficult decisions you should be making immediately. We take that to mean that if you're finding it hard to make decisions about your marketing as you go along then you're probably doing it right, because marketing isn't easy and the decisions are important[2]. The worst thing you can do is ignore the decisions until they become too urgent to deal with effectively.

Every time you make a decision about spending time and money on a customer, you are investing in the future of your business and hoping for a return. When the return comes, it's a vindication of your decision. If it doesn't come, then you simply have to make another decision. What you can't do is wait and wait for things to happen.

Let us repeat. Monitor and measure everything you can and be as sensitive and light on your feet as possible. If you don't get the right response – go back to your plans, work out why and change.

It's all going horribly RIGHT!

Growth changes everything. If your personal plan doesn't include your love of a challenge or your ambition to be the director of a bigger company (as opposed to, say, experimenting with new flavours of ice cream) then you have to face the fact; this isn't the same business.

Of course its value to you may be so much that you never want to let go. It's a difficult decision to let go of the golden goose.

In which case you will have to get some very good people in to keep it running while you learn a new job (being the CEO or even chairman) and make your new plans. If you don't want to do that, you might still have to get some very good people in to keep it running and then decide on your own future. The business may be saleable and you may have other personal ambitions.

Selling your pride and joy isn't the end of the road. We know of several entrepreneurs who built up profitable businesses that were sold as going concerns. Each of them gained thousands (in one case millions) of pounds which, after a suitable pause, enabled them to start a business all over again. In some cases these new companies were in competition with the old one!

The point here was that the owners concerned were less comfortable with a mature business than with a new, small and growing business. They knew their strengths and what motivated them, and they stuck to it.

Growth isn't always good news. When you set out your aims, what was the scale of growth you imagined? Sometimes it's simply being able to pay for you to work in your own business full time. But more than one small business owner has described 'suddenly' finding themselves responsible for three, tens or hundreds of other workers.

The change also brings about different challenges. Not the least of these is the inability of the company to finance the increased levels of work going through and a cash crisis. This specific problem is dealt with at length in Bob Gorton's excellent book on selling[3].

As we've said, growth also means your role changes and the skills you had may become redundant. We hope that some of the concepts and skills we've worked through in this book stand you in good stead for a period of (controlled) growth. Indeed, it may be that you grow as your business grows so that you relish the challenges of managing your burgeoning empire.

One thing we believe is essential in any business owner is a willingness to learn. Some entrepreneurs are 'sponges' that learn from anyone and everyone about their industry, about technology, in fact about every aspect of business. Others have to work hard to network and search out ideas and knowledge that can benefit their company.

The excitement of magnolia emulsion . . .

We can usually tell when a business has been taken over by someone without business experience. Not for them the slick overnight refit with the minimum amount of fuss.

A shop that takes four weeks to fit out loses money for a month. The novice usually fails to plan the refit adequately and is at the mercy of the small builder they employed (on price of course).

The owner spends days fretting over the wall colours or the finish on the shelves while their spare cash ebbs away.

Really successful retailers don't want to tie up their resources unnecessarily. So if you are expanding into new premises or opening a new branch, then do it on the understanding that it's better to have the shop open and selling rather than getting just the right shade of specially imported Italian marble on the countertop.

By picking up this book, we hope you have identified yourself as someone who is hungry to learn and open to new ideas. If you are prepared to take a (measured) risk, then you might also realise your dream of owning and running the business you have in mind.

Keeping yourself on track

Everybody allows their attention to wander sometimes. If we struggle to pay attention to the TV or a website for more than 40 seconds, how can we possibly keep an eye on our business for years at a time?

While it is now obvious to you that you need to make customers the centre of your business, the day-to-day reality of business is that you (and the people who work with you) can fall into a routine. The doors to the shop are opened, the factory starts up, you switch on the computer, or you get in the car to go and track down business.

It's too easy for the work to become grey and uniform. And when you're unexcited by your business, how can customers be even remotely interested . . . let alone interested enough to pay you? Here are a number of ways of making your business more than just a job.

Involve your people

Almost every business benefits from a daily briefing for everyone – especially when there are daily targets. One business we know encouraged staff to arrive early and made sure they were given breakfast on the premises. It was a great moment to chat with everyone and completely unlike some of the (infrequent and therefore dreaded) 'boss's talks' we have witnessed, where staff are told that if sales don't pick up, their jobs are on the line.

Don't make your staff think about their next career – ask them their advice about this one. Don't tell them you have a problem – ask them for *three* solutions and reward them. Above all, find every opportunity to share with them your inspiring vision for the company.

Give time over to other people's ideas

Please don't have a suggestion box. It's just an inadequate nod towards consultation. Remember that much of the knowledge of your business and your customers resides in the heads of those who work for you. Such knowledge only has value when it is put to work and is shared.

Allow people to pursue their ideas – at least until they can prove their value. You don't have time to do their work as well as your own, so work out how you can give them the freedom to make the job better/more efficient/more profitable.

Take time out

Try and give yourself, and others, time to think and develop. Some of the best companies allow people some time off for hobbies or volunteering. One company we know gives everyone a modest budget to spend on learning a new skill – it doesn't have to be work related either. It's just an attempt to give employees reasons to be glad they work for you and a sense of being valued. This is then reflected in their work with customers (see page 181).

The same should apply to you. Don't feel guilty if, every so often, you hide away with the phone off to *really* think about your business and to get out those old scribbled notes (not forgetting the hairy potato!) to take stock.

Invite people in

Never forget either that your very best customers can be made to feel part of the company too. Breaking down the 'us and them' barrier can energise your company. What happens if customers are routinely invited to see their work being produced? What happens if you have a 'supplier day' every quarter, when everyone can meet the voices at the other end of the telephone?

If the worst should happen

Closing down a business is never easy. It's even more painful when you are forced into liquidation.

Trust us; it's not the end of the world.

You should aim to be as professional in the winding-up of your business as you tried to be when it was starting. Call on your suppliers and give them the full facts. Thank them and apologise.

You should also communicate with your customers, thanking them for their support and, if you can, helping them to make alternative arrangements.

There is always the possibility that you will be in a position to start up again or to join in partnership with someone else in the same business.

The relationships you worked so hard to build up are valuable assets you should try to maintain.

Find a mentor

Having someone to talk with about your business, who will respect your confidence and who has no axe to grind, is invaluable. An experienced business person, even if she doesn't know your industry, can give you a new perspective on any problem that confronts you. Don't just call on your mentor in times of trouble though – that's not what the relationship is for. Meet regularly and don't postpone because of a business crisis – this is your job, no-one else's.

Mentor yourself too

Never stop reviewing the progress of your corporate and personal plan – are you getting there? Start with your own motivation. One technique we have suggested is a kind of 'cue card' or a 'mantra' that is pinned above your desk or is on the desktop of your PC.

You can then read it at the start of the day or when you're faced with an important decision. It's like the equivalent of a personal coach or a personal trainer, the quiet word in the ear that motivates you to do better. It can be a reminder of your 'purpose'.

Always plan as if you're starting the business again

As a business start-up you don't have any customers, so you don't take them for granted. If you constantly go back to the first principles of your plan and check to see if they still hold good, then you will always be thinking strategically rather than flying on autopilot. No-one else in the company will take responsibility for those long-term important things, so you must. The plan you have developed must be constantly revised and renewed.

Each year you will write another plan, each one more refined than the last and, we hope, each more successful than the previous year's. It's probably true to say that your plan will take all year to write and all the following year to rewrite. It's a never-ending process, but you learn so much as you go through it, both about yourself and about your customers.

Do you know how long it took to write *this* book?

Much of what you have read is based on over 40 years of working and studying marketing. Forty years between us, that is. In that time, our joint view of marketing has changed from one of awe to one of (some would say) thinly veiled contempt.

But marketing is a powerful concept, especially for the small business that really gets to grips with it. Unfortunately many don't.

The reasons for writing this book were threefold.

Firstly, of course, it was shameless self-promotion. In our everyday lives, having our names on a publication (especially with such a prestigious publisher as Bloomsbury) does us no end of good.

Secondly (and more seriously), we genuinely see many small businesses struggle with marketing. It's not that there aren't smiling consultants and agencies out there ready to take their money and tell them to rewrite their mission statement or produce some innovative advertising. There are plenty of those. Nor is it the lack of marketing textbooks or training programmes – if anything there are too many.

No, the problem is that business people themselves find it hard to know when they are being sold to (by those consultants, agencies and marketing authors) and when *they* should be calling the shots.

We find that some of the basic (but tricky) questions in the first half of this book often go unanswered by the companies we visit. They don't know why they are in business, they don't know what they are selling and, crucially, they don't really understand much about their customers. And that means that they really can't implement marketing as the books dictate, or even ask the professionals for the kind of help they need. We'd like to think a fairly readable book might help.

The third reason for writing is to hand over to people like you some of the power. Best practice in business isn't confined to multinationals; in fact there is an increasing trend for big companies to try and act like small ones and to encourage individual entrepreneurship. You are in a position to write the rules for *your* business as you go along, with a bit of a helping hand.

Tell us what you find out

We accept that some of the examples may not have led you to Damascene revelations; that's OK. These are small businesses that haven't changed the world. However, as we said at the beginning, it's often by thinking about them again and even re-writing your own 'what if?' scenario that you begin to see things differently. If you do so, or your own story is illustrative of what we've said, then feel free to send it to us at *www.pleasewalkonthegrass.com* and we'll consider using it in a future edition.

Conversely, if you think we've made a mistake, then still get in touch in the same way. Much as we like to pretend otherwise, we are not infallible and we'd like to put things right. We'd also like to use your experience and insight for the benefit of other readers.

If you follow the principles we've set out and make a million, gifts can also be sent to us. If you try to follow the principles in this book and fall flat on your face ... we'll be in Buenos Aires.

What next?

With any luck, you no longer feel the need to sign up for that one-day course on 'understanding the principles of marketing'. If you've been working as we suggested, pen and paper to hand, you should have a plan of your business and how it is going to recruit and keep customers. You will also have an idea of what is involved and, frankly, how hard it is to accomplish and so be alert to the need to track everything.

We'd like to finish with one final secret which we'd like to share . . .

Marketing doesn't work.

Marketing doesn't take a company or a product and make it famous or successful. Marketing can't allow you to sit back and watch the money roll in. Marketing is not the elixir of business life.

But marketing is, or should be, a state of mind where everything that you do with your business is built on the inescapable truth that it's your customers who pay your wages. Marketing itself doesn't work – *your* marketing might.

Notes/ References

1. Cressy, R. (2006). 'Why do Most Firms Die Young?', *Small Business Economics*, 26.
2. Seth Godin again – in his 2006 publication *Small Is the New Big* (*www. sethgodin.com/small*).
3. Gorton, B. (2011). *Boosting Sales on a Shoestring*, Bloomsbury Publishing Plc.

For more information

Look at the Toolkits online at *www.acblack.com/business*. You can also contact the authors via *www.pleasewalkonthegrass.com*.

INDEX